HOW TO SHU[...] YOUR BS FACTORY

BREAK THE MOULD

VOLUME 2

TIM ROBERTS

This book is for Joyno, Phoebe & Lucie –
you're the reason I work my arse off &
why I have to shut down my BS Factory.

And for Dusty & Tigger – our mad mogs
who bring us so much joy.

To my mate Budgie – love you Craigy baby.

Keep smiling. Keep being you.

To Claire

Hope you enjoy reading the book & shutting down your BS Factory :)

keep smiling
keep being you

[illegible]

67% of workers feel they work in a toxic environment.

74% of workers say their mental health at work is poor or fair.

2024 report on mental health in the workplace

https://monsterworkwatch24.my.canva.site/monster-poll-mental-health-in-the-workplace-2024

'And let the echoes of joy keep
shining on through
Believe in yourself and you can
make a difference
Believe in yourself and you can
find a second chance
You know you gotta wake up
wake up in time
And don't let life pass you by.'

– STONE FOUNDATION

TABLE OF CONTENTS

THIS BOOK IS FOR...

Spoiler alert – that sentence will be finished in the same way it will be finished in all of my books... This book is for *you*. It is for you because It Always Starts With You.

- Do you want to wake up on a Monday morning and actually be excited about going to work?
- Do you want to feel better about yourself?
- Have you had enough of self-doubt and imposter syndrome?
- Are you fed up with having bad days at work?
- Do you want to feel confident and self-assured?
- Do you want to be a more naturally inspiring leader?

- Are you sick of other people's (and your own!) BS getting in your way?

This book is for the people who are held back by their negative thoughts and feelings. It is for the leaders who care and who want to make work better for themselves and their teams. It is for anyone with an inner critic. It is for anyone who has experienced a crisis of confidence. It is for anyone who has been in a situation that beat the shit out of them and left them despondent at the world. It is for the teams who want to do good work and work in a positive environment. It is for the organisations who want their culture to be one of engagement and positivity.

This book is for all of you.

THIS BOOK WILL...

Introduce you to your Bullshit Factory and show you how to shut it down. After reading this book, you will no longer be overrun with negative thoughts and feelings. It will save you from falling into negative attitudes and behaviours that aren't really you. It will show you how to have the positive impact you want to have on yourself and those you lead. Most of all, this book will show you how to choose a positive response to all the BS thrown at you, whether it's coming from others or even yourself. Because if there's one thing in life that's guaranteed it's that there's always BS thrown at you, either by yourself or others. You can never go too long without it, so that's why you need to be ready. Then you can know how to shake it off without getting caught up in it. It's THE life skill we all need.

Just stop and think for a moment:

- What would it be like to be free of negative thoughts and feelings?
- What do you actually need to do to be free?

This book will show you how to be more confident, how you can be your true, authentic self and have more good days than bad days. It will stop you feeling powerless and instead empower you to be the person and the leader you want to be. I am really passionate about helping you to Break the Mould and be confident in just being you.

We will start with the personal development and show you how your Bullshit Factory invades your thoughts and feelings. We will then explore it in a business context and show how the Bullshit Factory invades what we do at work. We'll look at the profound impact that your Bullshit Factory has on you and how that seeps into what leaders and teams do. Because what your Bullshit Factory does to you, you take into work and we have to be able to shut it down personally to turn that profound impact into a positive one for you and those whom you lead and work with.

Most importantly, this book will give you the most powerful ability that a human being can have – the ability to choose a positive response to your thoughts and feelings.

Right now, you don't even know what your Bullshit Factory is and that likely means that you are buying into all of the crappy products that it produces. Those crappy products are what ruin your days. You don't ruin your days; your Bullshit Factory does.

This book is going to take you from having the kind of days where you wake up with a sense of dread about what lies ahead to the days when you wake up feeling good about yourself, the tasks you face and feeling confident that you can deal with whatever shit gets thrown at you. Even on the days when you wake up in a stinking mood, the confidence and techniques you will gain from this book will mean that you will be able to turn it into a good day for you.

By the end of the book, you will know exactly what your Bullshit Factory is, why you have one, how its BS holds you back and how to shut it down so its crappy products no longer dictate how you think and feel about yourself and what happens to you. This book will show you how to challenge yourself so you can build the confidence to be who you want to be.

Warning: this is NOT just another one of those "cool" books with a unique view on how your feelings work that you love reading and recommend to everyone but actually end up doing nothing with other than repeat throwaway phrases from it, saying things like *"oh yeah, it's your Bullshit Factory, isn't it?"* or *"you better shut down your Bullshit Factory!"* only to then allow it to keep doing what it does anyway. It is not another corporate or academic book that is only published to make money for some self-appointed expert that doesn't actually give a shit about you. I give a shit about you and will show you how to give a shit about you too.

We are going to do some big, exciting work together. We'll explore and challenge the darker side of your inner critic and peer into those shadowy corners where your Bullshit Factory operates. I promise to help you to recognise your own negativity and give you the courage and tools to challenge and overcome it. I will keep that promise by giving you heightened self-awareness and techniques that are fun, no-nonsense and easy to adopt.

Starting this book, you might have some trepidation about what is ahead or expect it to be hard work. It's not going to be hard work with a good few laughs along the way. You're about to complete a journey of self-exploration so you can see the Bullshit Factory for what it is and stop it in its tracks.

'Better stop dreaming of the quiet life
Cause it's the one we'll never know.
And quit running for that runaway bus.
'Cause those rosy days are few
And stop apologising for the
things you've never done
'Cause time is short and life is cruel
but it's up to us to change.'

– THE JAM

I might sound like I am getting on my soapbox a bit (I'm writing a book, so if I can't get on my soapbox now when the hell can I?) but that's because I believe passionately in what this book is all about – your emotional intelligence, which will get you further in life than anything else.

I stand firmly on my soapbox because, for many, many years, my Bullshit Factory was in full force, holding me back and making me a right miserable sod. I don't want that to happen to you. I want you to feel the freedom and have the confidence that comes with shutting down your Bullshit Factory.

'When your head is so full
And you feel misunderstood
And the fear is coming fast
You think your time has passed
You say why me, why me?'

– RICHARD ASHCROFT

And I've not even told you the best bit yet... You don't need a psychology degree or the ability to understand the inner workings of the human brain to shut down your Bullshit Factory. If we haven't met yet, then one of the first things you need to know about me is that I am a straight-talking Northerner, so you'll get no academic jargon or "psycho-babble" here. Everything we do together in the book is straightforward, in your control and easy to understand.

Most people reading this book won't care about the intimate operations of an amygdala or your prefrontal cortex. Like them, you care about you. You care about being able to stop beating yourself up. You care about being able to wake up in the morning and feel good about yourself and your day ahead.

I wrote this book because my Bullshit Factory came very close to ruining my life and I don't want anyone else to go through that.

'Living is easy with eyes closed
Misunderstanding all you see
It's getting hard to be someone,
but it all works out.'

– THE BEATLES

MEET TIM ROBERTS

Tim Roberts is:

- A father, husband and Mod before anything else.
- A leadership coach who develops authentic and emotionally intelligent leaders.
- Sick of people suffering at the hands of their Bullshit Factory.
- One of the most engaging and inspirational coaches out there. If you don't work with him after reading this book then your Bullshit Factory has won!
- Here to coach you to make positive choices.

Tim has:

- Inspired thousands of people to be their true, authentic selves.
- Already written a really good book – *Break the Mould - volume 1*.

- Had enough of decent people being beaten down by BS.
- A unique no BS approach to coaching.
- A firmly held belief that It Always Starts With You.

Follow Tim via:
www.enthusecoaching.com

www.linkedin.com/in/timrobertsenthuse/

How to Shut Down Your Bullshit Factory Workbook

I have created a free workbook to help you to shut down your Bullshit Factory. This includes all of the coaching questions that you will be asked throughout the book and space to capture your thoughts and reflections. It also drives you to action to shut down your Bullshit Factory by including the techniques I share in the book.

Head to my website by scanning the QR code below to download the workbook and use whilst reading the book.

PREFACE

"YOU'RE A COMPLETE PRICK, TIM"

'I may get it wrong sometimes
but I come back in style.'

– THE STYLE COUNCIL

London, 25th September, 2018 and I am buzzing. The late summer sun is shining and I am in a pub, the kind of pub that only exists in London, having a cold beer and preparing to appear at my biggest public speaking gig to date at DisruptHR London in front of 200 people.

I have prepared and I feel ready and want to unleash my no bullshit approach to public speaking on the great people of England's capital (or at least the ones who had bought a ticket!).

This is a massive opportunity for me as I prepare to leave the dickheads behind and launch my own coaching business. I have worked my arse off for the last five years to be in this position. I've practised my talk and feel confident.

I take a moment in the pub to take it all in... I am sitting in a cool London pub drinking nice beer with two of my mates (hello Kelly Swingler and Jo Byrne) about to go on stage and keep building momentum towards what I really want to do. I live for this kind of shit! Some people run a mile from public speaking, I thrive on it.

"Sup up your beer and collect your fags" (if you know, you know) is the cry as we leave the pub and head over to the venue. Bring it on.

'There will always be suffering
It flows through life like water.'

– NICK CAVE AND THE BAD SEEDS

Fast forward one hour...

"Get out of here now, Tim – pretend you're going to the loo and just don't come back."

"You're an idiot. Everyone here thinks you're an idiot."

"You've messed it all up."

"Don't even look at anyone. You're not good enough to be here."

"Why the fuck did you ever think that you could do this? You're a complete prick, Tim."

Those were some of my thoughts after I had finished my first DisruptHR inspirational talk. It all started so well and I was in my flow, getting laughs in the right places and the audience was engaging with me.

And then disaster struck. I tripped over a cable on stage, disconnecting the feed to the screen and taking the host's laptop flying across the stage. In front of 200 people remember.

If I had asked myself before my talk "*what is the worst thing that could happen?*", this would have been up there. Not only did I properly trip and nearly go face-first onto the stage, I completely wiped out the host's laptop, taking it off the table it was on and sending it flying across the stage as the screen went blank.

People from the venue scrambled around to reconnect the screen and after a few awkward minutes (it felt like an hour) of me padding by saying some nonsense on stage, I got the thumbs up to continue. I embarrassingly finished my talk without the gusto I had before. I ruined it all with my clumsiness and got a smattering of applause from a previously rapt audience.

'I wanna wake up
And feel better 'bout me
But you make me feel
You're my enemy.'

– STEREOPHONICS

I trudged off stage and I stood there in the auditorium surrounded by my peers sweating, getting all flushed and hating myself. I was the second speaker of the night and had to stand there watching as more speakers took to the stage and delivered their talks without tripping over or wrecking the set-up.

I couldn't wait for the break so I could get out of there. Despite there being other speakers on, I couldn't take in anything they were saying. It was one of those moments, where everyone around you is enjoying themselves and you feel like you don't belong and it's as if you're not really there.

I was completely lost to my negative thoughts and feelings. I felt like everyone was looking at me thinking *what a dickhead* and *why is he still here?,* which can be most articulately summarised with the thought I kept returning to: *"You're a complete prick, Tim"*.

Those 20 minutes between my talk and the break felt like an eternity. I made my escape plan and was fixated on the time so that when the break arrived and people moved from their seats, I could quickly head to the exit and never look back. Never to go on stage again. Get back to where I belong – as a nobody.

'Don't have to swim with the tide
Swim against the tide and find
some hand to hold
Find somebody to show the light.'

– RICHARD ASHCROFT

Before I'd taken two steps, I was halted in my tracks and embraced by a woman that I'd never met before.

"You were amazing. Your talk was brilliant and made so much sense and the way you handled your little trip was unbelievable. I'd have cried if that happened to me, and you just took it all in your stride. I had to come and say hello and well done before you get mobbed."

And mobbed I was! People were queueing up to talk to me. To me, the dickhead who just tripped over on stage and delayed the whole event whilst the host awkwardly reconnected everything.

I remember a big man with a ginger beard coming up to me and hugging me so much that my feet came off the floor as he boomed, *"Best fucking talk ever mate. It's about time someone called out all the crap that people spout about learning and development"*. He didn't even mention my stage fall!

A less animated man followed the bearded man by shaking my hand and simply saying, *"I really enjoyed that. Thank you."*

The bit that totally blew my mind and left me feeling totally staggered was when the speaker who went after me came up to me and told me, *"You were fantastic. I can't believe I had to follow you!"* I took the compliment and told them I really enjoyed their talk, even though I hadn't even noticed them on stage because my head was completely up my arse at that point.

I'd like to apologise here and now to whoever that speaker was who followed me for lying to them! That's what negative thoughts and feelings do to a man who is totally consumed by his Bullshit Factory.

'Keep telling the same old lies.
Repeat, repeat, repeat.'

– STONE FOUNDATION

You see, the voice inside my head, or rather my Bullshit Factory, made me forget that my talk was a great talk. I engaged people, they laughed out loud and my ideas were new and original. And as for the trip, that made me even more memorable because of the way, and I quote another audience member, *"I styled it out and didn't give up"*.

Yet, in the moment, my Bullshit Factory had me believing that everyone hated me and that I had ruined their evening and ruined my reputation as an inspirational speaker. If I had listened to my Bullshit Factory that night, I would never have got on stage again. I would have gone back to a job that I hated and never have created Enthuse Coaching and Break the Mould. I definitely wouldn't be writing this book if I had let my Bullshit Factory win!

'There is more in a smile than in a hand.'

– THE VERVE

I laugh about it now (if you want to laugh at it too, search online for "Tim Roberts DisruptHR London"), and I have gone on to speak at other DisruptHR events and do many more inspirational talks to bigger crowds at company conferences and big industry events.

This all goes to show that we survive these moments and our negative perception in these moments is a million miles away from what the other people there are actually thinking and feeling towards you. We live another day to do another inspirational talk and keep doing what we love doing... so we can embarrass ourselves all over again! And sometimes the things that cause us the most embarrassment create the most positive influence on others.

That is just one example where my Bullshit Factory threatened to determine what happened to me. This experience alone could have fuelled my Bullshit Factory for years to come, preventing me from ever speaking in public again. And mine wouldn't just explode in specific circumstances; it was often a constant for me before I learned to shut it down. You see, your Bullshit Factory can sabotage you whenever it wants!

“Your Bullshit Factory can sabotage you whenever it wants!”

I want to take you on a journey to understand what your Bullshit Factory does to you and how you can shut it down. Whether it's triggered by specific circumstances or whether your Bullshit Factory is a constant, let's shut that fucker down together.

Why? Because I am sick of good people feeling bad about themselves. Being sabotaged by their own Bullshit; holding themselves back from being who they are and doing what they really want to do.

The first thing to remember as you start reading this book – your negative thoughts and feelings aren't you. They are examples of your Bullshit Factory working hard against you, and together we're going to win our battles and make positive choices so you can believe in yourself again.

'You gotta keep on keeping on
No matter how hard it is
You gotta keep on keeping on
No matter how rough it gets
You gotta keep on keeping on.'

– NOLAN PORTER

PART ONE

IT ALWAYS STARTS WITH YOU

CHAPTER ONE

PLEASE ALLOW ME TO INTRODUCE MYSELF...I'M YOUR BULLSHIT FACTORY

'Pleased to meet you
Hope you guess my name
But what's puzzling you
Is the nature of my game.'

– THE ROLLING STONES

So, what actually is your Bullshit Factory?

It's the part of you that generates negative thoughts and feelings. It leads you to criticise and doubt yourself. It causes you to make bad decisions and ultimately stops you from being who you really are and doing what you really want to do. It makes you behave in a negative way and adopt negative attitudes.

In this chapter, I will introduce you to your Bullshit Factory, show you why it exists and how it works. I will expose you to the Bullshit all around us that fuels your Bullshit Factory. This chapter will set the tone as we bring the Bullshit Factory into your consciousness and spark your motivation to shut it down. What you're about to read might shock you and it will also make you think about you and your own experiences. It will make you embrace yourself as a human being, along with all your faults, so you can see that the negativity inside of you is NOT you… it is your Bullshit Factory.

'I've been right,
I've been a fool
I've been bright,
I've been uncool

You hate me, you love me
I'm only judged by myself.'

– ERIC CANTONA

Imagine a factory in your mind, relentlessly churning out faulty products every day, and you will see your Bullshit Factory. It starts by churning out those pesky negative thoughts and feelings which then go through the assembly line and spit out your negative self-talk that nags away at you, telling you that you are no good. Next off the assembly line comes your negative self-image which makes you feel like you look bad at what you do and gives you the gift of pessimism. All of these elements are put in the mixture and create your gloom-ridden anticipation, which makes you think and feel that every day is going to be a bad day. And then voila... off your Bullshit Factory assembly line rolls your reactive, negative attitudes and behaviours.

What starts with your thoughts and feelings produces your behaviours and attitudes. They are the products of your Bullshit Factory that other people see and judge you for. The kind of behaviours it produces are not the ones you would actually choose for yourself and often leave you with a sense of regret. The attitudes that get produced by your Bullshit Factory infect your mindset, making it gloomy, pessimistic and cynical. Although these products are shoddy, your Bullshit Factory is brilliant at marketing and does an unbelievable job at selling its BS to you. It makes the crappy products feel exciting and seduces you into a spiral of negativity.

Here's where it takes control and starts running and ruining your life...

Despite the fact it is selling you faulty products, you go back for more and more. You believe that the BS is right for you and you buy into it and act on the BS. That's because it's generally easier to do that than fighting against it. Even though your Bullshit Factory makes you do bad things, those bad things are often an easy choice. It's easier to wallow in self-pity than tackle it head on. It's easier to micromanage your team than to have difficult conversations with them. It's easier to keep doing what you've always done rather than learn how to do new things and change yourself.

'Seasons change but some people never do.'

– FUTURE ISLANDS

Stop and consider for a moment the times when:

- You have been riddled with negative thoughts and feelings.
- Your self-doubt has prevented you from doing something you want to do.
- You are consumed by a negative, self-fulfilling prophecy that your day ahead will be bad.
- Your attitudes and behaviours have let you down.

None of the above are you – they are your Bullshit Factory. It infects everything you do and takes advantage of your humanness by turning your experiences into a maelstrom of negativity.

Amongst other things, my Bullshit Factory tells me:

- I am a bad parent.
- I am not as good as other coaches.
- This book will be shit.
- I should forget about achieving my dreams and ambitions and "just get a job".

And that's on a good day! When I have a setback, like a potential client turning me down for work, my Bullshit Factory scoffs and tells me that I will never work again.

'I wouldn't treat a friend like I treat myself.'

– STEREOPHONICS

Your Bullshit Factory is what stops you applying for the job you want and from sharing your ideas. It blocks you from living the life you want to lead. It is what turns decent human beings into micromanagers and tells you that something that hasn't happened yet is going to go badly. It is the part of you that self-sabotages and holds you back. It drives your comparisons, telling you that other people are better than you, know more than you and are having a better time than you. It blindfolds you from seeing just how good you really are and the value you bring to others.

'Am I good enough? Am I a good man? Am I a good father? Everyone asks themselves these questions. Well... unless you're a dickhead.'

– PAUL WELLER

Why is it called a Bullshit Factory?

Because what it produces is complete and utter Bullshit! It is as simple as that. Although like most BS, it is incredibly persuasive and can convince you that its faulty goods are right for you.

I'm not writing a psychological opus or erudite academic thesis here, I am writing something simple to help you to overcome your negative thoughts and feelings and choose positive attitudes and behaviours. I choose to call it your Bullshit Factory because no-one actually wants what it produces yet we buy into it time and time again.

You can call it what you want. Call it your inner critic, your moral compass or the devil on your shoulder. Call it fucking Bob if you want to. What I want to help you with is being who you want to be and not allowing your Bullshit Factory to determine what your experience of work and life is.

No-one wants to be miserable or stressed. No-one wants to be the person at work who others avoid and talk about behind their back. No-one wants to be the dickhead boss. No-one wants to feel worthless and incapable. No-one wants to be riddled with self-doubt or feel anxious. No-one wants to be Neggy Nelly or Dave Downer. No-one wants a life full of Bullshit. Yet all of us have either been those things or we know people who have!

Here are some examples of what comes out of your Bullshit Factory and into your consciousness: -

- ➡ Apathy
- ➡ Arrogance
- ➡ Bravado
- ➡ Complacency
- ➡ Disrespect
- ➡ Ego
- ➡ Ignorance
- ➡ Imposter Syndrome
- ➡ Inferiority
- ➡ Insecurity
- ➡ Jealousy
- ➡ Low self-esteem
- ➡ Self-loathing
- ➡ Shame
- ➡ Uncertainty

I have never met anyone yet who actually wants any of those things but I have seen them pop up in every single workplace I have been to. And if you don't shut down yours, you will get all the Bullshit that you don't want. Furthermore, it's not just you who suffers – you'll be generously spreading that BS around with your family, friends and workmates.

Before we move on, it is really important to make something clear here – the trigger for your negative thoughts and feelings will always be there. Bad things will happen in life and your Bullshit Factory will always latch on to them. Even the most outwardly confident people have a Bullshit Factory piping up every now and then trying to sabotage them. You can't control or change that. What you can control is how you choose to respond to it, how you react to the BS it is waving under your nose and trying to convince you is real. That is how you shut it down. I want you to embrace your Bullshit Factory; let's see it in broad daylight for what it is and then focus on choosing how to positively respond.

Whilst your Bullshit Factory produces the biggest challenges that we face as a human, you can shut it down by developing and applying the greatest power you have as a human being: how you choose to positively respond to your thoughts and feelings.

'Everything is taking shape
and going to plan
How quickly though, life can turn around
One step forward, two steps back
He's lost in the crowd
Oh, we stand together, we fall
Just know that belief conquers all.'

– TOM GRENNAN

Bullshit is all around you, it's everywhere you go

Negative things driven by people's Bullshit factories happen around us all the time. Days at work can feel like you're surrounded by negativity, even when you're working from home! Just consider the Bullshit that has been put out there every day for hundreds of years by newspapers or in corporate PR.

And the wonderful 21st century phenomenon of social media. For all of its ability to connect people around the world and the positive "influencers" out there, your "feed" can be full of bullshit. This comes either from people sharing emotionally driven things that their Bullshit Factory tells them to post, only to later wish that they had never shared them with the world, or from the algorithms that someone who doesn't know you or care about you chooses to place on your screen.

My Bullshit Factory loves a bit of comparison to keep me feeling small. It can tell me that I am rubbish at my job and that no-one likes me just because I see other coaches sharing their work on LinkedIn and getting more likes than my posts do. It even does it when I see my friends having a good time on social media.

I remember going into a spiral of sadness and envy because I saw multiple posts from friends on a night out. A night out that I had declined to attend because it was at the last place I would ever want to visit. Yet when my Bullshit Factory sees that, it tells me that I am a bad friend and my life is pointless. I've also got mates who post their wonderful life on Facebook and then, when we go for a pint together, they spend hours moaning about their wife and telling me how much they hate their job – yet more BS from the Bullshit Factory.

I am the first to admit that for many years I was one of the parents who told the world through my social posts that my kids are perfect. I love my kids to death but they still ruin the odd meal out and have the odd seismic meltdown in the supermarket. However, those things never made it into my posts because my Bullshit Factory told me that would cause embarrassment and make me look like a bad parent, so self-preservation kicked in and I only told the world about the good things that happened.

Social media companies embody this kind of bullshit. They tell us from their shiny offices how they want to connect the world and make us more creative when all they really want to do is make billions of dollars from marketing revenue and flogging your data for more people to send you bullshit e-mails and ads.

On top of all of that, you have the pressure of comparison telling us that we have to be slim, have a six-pack, own materialistic things, go on the best holidays, have the best lips and lashes. Worse than that, the biggest one of all, we tell ourselves to adopt other people's beliefs and agree with their political persuasions and other preferences that have nothing to do with you.

'Now if there's a smile on my face
It's only there trying to fool the public.'

– SMOKEY ROBINSON

"The more bullshit you let into your heart and mind, the more your Bullshit Factory takes over"

The bullshit from the world pervades our consciousness, we somehow pick up on its criticism and internalise that we should "be" a certain way. The more bullshit you let into your heart and mind, the more your Bullshit Factory takes over. It starts to tell us how to behave and even how to dress and how we think about ourselves through the lens of the world's bullshit.

I remember going to work with a group of graduates for the first time at a global insurance company in London's finance district. I absolutely panicked in my hotel room the night before after I read up on the company and perused their website; it made me start looking at what time nearby clothes shops opened so I could buy a more suitable outfit based on what I expected them to be like!

I had gone properly geared up with my burgundy loafers, Prince of Wales checked trousers, knitted navy polo shirt and a cool overshirt – the way I love to dress and the clothes I feel good in. Yet, here I was thinking I needed to completely change my outfit (and therefore, change myself) just because my Bullshit Factory believed the hype on their website. It started to tell me that the graduate group were going to be much smarter than me and cooler than me because they were younger. They would not dig me at all because of my age, the way I dressed and my Northern accent.

After a sleepless night, with my Bullshit Factory making me toss and turn, I went to work with a feeling of dread in the pit of my stomach. I got a valuable reminder that my world can be full of bullshit as it turned out that the graduate group was fantastic to work with. They were keen to learn from me, took the piss out of me (in a nice way that I appreciated), but they also showed their respect because I was the oldest in the room and, most importantly, because of how I talked. They lapped up my content and told me my approach was different and much better than the death by PowerPoint that they were used to, sharing their appreciation at the end of the day.

A great day all round. Imagine if I had allowed my Bullshit Factory to ruin that for me, if I had let it stop me being myself and sent me to some bland clothes shop to pick up the corporate uniform of chinos, light blue shirt, suit blazer and brogues?!! This could have been another "brown shoes moment" all over again for me! (check out *Break the Mould – volume 1* if you don't know my brown shoes story.)

It was a classic reminder that you are always at risk of bullshit ruining your day and, more importantly, that the truth is often not as bad as your fears.

'Oh, baby you're the only
thing in this whole world
That's pure and good and right
And wherever you are
and wherever you go
There's always gonna be some light.'

– MEAT LOAF

The BSF also filters into the ridiculous. You've got the everyday ridiculous things that people repeatedly say. A couple of my favourites are: -

"Don't eat too many bananas in one day – it's the potassium." This BS comes from the risk of eating more than 30 bananas in one day which could potentially give you a heart attack. Apart from Bananaman on a really busy day who the fuck has ever eaten more than 30 bananas in one day?

"Cheese gives you nightmares." This complete BS gets retold because cheese is hard to digest so eating it late at night leads to a restless night's sleep; there is zero proof that it actually causes nightmares. There has never been a news report saying that the entire UK population has ruined

their Boxing Day due to nightmares after nailing an entire cheese board on Christmas night. It's feeling fat as piss from eating it that ruins your sleep, not the cheese itself!!

And the ones that filter into work such as *"people who work from home are lazy"* and *"I haven't got time for that leadership development stuff"*. These iterations of BS come out of people's gobs thanks to the Bullshit Factory making people want to know every detail of what other people are doing. And the avoidance of personal development is a classic trait of your BSF keeping you secure in your comfort zone of not admitting your vulnerabilities.

People repeat these things without any awareness that it is just coming from the world's Bullshit Factory and how it makes them sound totally uninspired and uninteresting.

OK, they are relatively tame examples compared to the more severe Bullshit Factory driven behaviours I will be introducing you to later. Yet when we allow ourselves to voice or listen to this sort of bullshit, it encourages our own Bullshit Factory to keep producing it so, before you know it, you're either really boring or lost in a world believing utter shite that holds you back from being who you want to be and doing what you want to do. This is why I call it a Bullshit Factory, so you can see it for what it is, making sure that you and your life are driven by what you stand for and who you really are.

How would you rather spend your days, chatting shite or having a good time? The answer is obvious, but the way to achieve it is less so. The secret to having a good time lies in stopping the world's BS from firing up your own Bullshit Factory.

'You keep your mouth
in your backside baby
And you're using it daily in my defence.'

– SHED SEVEN

At this point I need to change how I refer to the Bullshit Factory for the remainder of the book. From this point forward, I will mainly use the acronym of BSF when talking about your Bullshit Factory. This is for three reasons: -

1. It saves you repeating three words when you already know what I am talking about.

2. It stops me worrying about being told off by my mum for using the word "Shit" hundreds of times in one book.

3. It will stop my publisher from stressing about the word count as BSF is one word compared to three which saves me a lot of word space over the entire book!

That's me shutting down my BSF right there as I have chosen not to worry about those three things and instead do something positive about them.

The BSF Production Cycle

'We've all been changed
from what we were
Our broken parts left
smashed off the floor.'

– EDITORS

Your BSF is a constant production line working away in your heart and mind. There are thousands of manufacturing companies out there that wish their production lines were as fast and as consistent as your BSF. It spits out its products at an alarming speed and can operate 24 hours a day for 365 days a year. It works on a cycle that takes over how you experience the world and how you think and feel about yourself. Infiltrating all the internal processes that are precious to you, it poisons your emotions, giving you BS perceptions of you, those around you and what is really happening.

Let me break down the BSF production line for you: -

1. It starts by producing some pretty uncomfortable **thoughts and feelings**.

2. This then moves on to producing negative **self-talk** (and you can be a right bastard to yourself).

3. Your pessimistic **self-image** comes next, making sure you don't think very much of yourself.

4. The penultimate stage produces a **gloom-ridden anticipation** of how things will go for you.

The end product of the BSF production line is...

5. Reactive **Attitudes** and **Behaviours** which are the products of your BSF as this is what everyone else sees.

This production line is part of you – it's what makes you human. I'll bring to life real examples of this production line that we can all relate to and show you how to shut yours down to release you from the vice-like grip of your BSF.

'And if at times it seems insane –
all the tears in searching;
Turning all your joy to pain.'

– PAUL WELLER

Why do we all have a BSF?

The first thing you need to understand about your BSF is that you're not the only one. We all have one. Everyone who reads this book, everyone you work with. Everyone you see on the street today, they all have their own BSF. And everyone is different, feeding off our own personal blend of doubts and fears. You will always have a BSF that's out of your control. What is in your control is how you reduce its production – it can literally go from being a mega factory to a tiny workshop in someone's shed.

The second thing you need to understand about the BSF is that because you are a human being this means that your thoughts and feelings will be automatically triggered by external events or how you expect future experiences to go for you. You have no control of that. We too are animals with primal instincts that take over in reaction to the situations that we face or expect to face.

As a human, you are built for survival which triggers a self-protection mechanism that stops you from taking risks and doing things differently. This self-protection mechanism can get out of control and consume you with negative emotions. Because your emotions are rocket fuel for your BSF, it is always switched on to what is going on around you and sends up an emotional flare to kick-start your production line.

My BSF regularly tells me that I'll *"get found out"* as a coach just because someone who didn't like me made a throwaway comment that I would last less than six months when I set up my own business because, and I quote: *"You're not corporate enough, Tim"*. Or going even further back into my personal vault of bullshit, I am genuinely scared of going to big social gatherings because I was bullied when I was at primary school and was often the butt of everyone's jokes in the playground. And even in my forties, my BSF tells me to anticipate it happening to me again.

Think about how many people get a new job that means the world to them and then, on your first day, you are riddled with self-doubt from imposter syndrome. Or the leader who works hard to get promoted and is then consumed with insecurity believing that everyone is out to get them. I dread to think how many people around the world, who are qualified and experienced to do their jobs, become obsessed with proving themselves thanks to their BSF giving them an inferiority complex. And let's not forget how many people get arrogance pumped out by their BSF making them think that they are God's gift when everyone else is thinking they are a total nobhead!

Having emotions and even negative thoughts and feelings is normal for you as a human. It can be a pattern of behaviour or something in-the-moment and it can take over your life and how you think and feel about yourself. But it is OK that you have negative thoughts and feelings. I have them too. It is OK that you have a BSF, I have one too. It keeps us on our toes and it works against us, especially in this modern world full of bullshit.

'Some people want the
rock without the roll
But we all know there's
no God without soul.'

– ARCADE FIRE

What powers your Bullshit Factory?

Us humans have many weird quirks. Weird because despite us being the dominant species on earth and having the most powerful and most valuable resource on our planet – our hearts and minds – it is the same hearts and minds that hold us back and make us experience self-doubt and even self-loathing. It confuses us, making our greatest strength feel like our major weakness when there is no actual real reason for it (it's bullshit, remember!). Your BSF grabs at these quirks and turns your natural human operating system into something that resembles the Death Star in Star Wars – something that only wants to destroy your entire existence.

'The past is our knowledge,
the present our mistake
And the future we always leave too late.'

– THE STYLE COUNCIL

In order to understand your BSF and ultimately shut it down, you need to embrace you as a primal human being and remember that the only difference between us and any other animal on earth is that we can think about our thoughts and feelings and choose what to do next.

No other animal on earth, no matter how smart or how cute they are, shares our greatest power of being able to choose how to positively respond to their thoughts and feelings. It is why our cat, the amazing and incomparable Tigger, will never ever use the toilet or wipe her own arse. Nor will she ever open the cupboard door and pour her food into a bowl to feed herself.

That unparalleled ability to reflect upon our thoughts and feelings and choose how we respond doesn't get enough praise or recognition. Instead, we focus on the skills and intelligence we need to do something and the expected outcomes that come from those things. This whips up our BSF to drive us to behaviours that lead to misery and disappointment.

Before we can unleash our greatest power and shut down our BSF, we need to better understand it and how it works. After all, it is fuelled by some simple elements of our human operating system.

'Guess it's life, doing its thing
Making you cry, making you think
Yeah life, dealing its hand
Making you cry and
you don't understand.'

– RICHARD ASHCROFT

The human fuel for your Bullshit Factory

1. Autopilot

First up is our autopilot – we think something, we feel something and then we do something. The first two parts of our autopilot are transient and sometimes it is the feeling (i.e. an extreme emotion) that comes first and we can end up doing something without even thinking. This autopilot is a huge strength for us as humans and, through learning and experience, our instincts give us our unconscious competence. You don't need to tell yourself to breathe, how to walk or to break suddenly when the wally in the BMW cuts you up on the motorway.

The danger here is when your BSF takes over your autopilot and tells you every day that you are not good enough or that the day ahead will be a bad one. This turns our strength into a weakness and we end up beating ourselves up and judging people around us. Our "unconscious competence" becomes something that attacks us every day.

A BSF-inspired autopilot makes you forget all the things that you are good at doing. Instead, it tells you things like *"you'll never get that job"*, leaving you stuck on an autopilot firmly fixed in the negativity zone and the action you take is to daydream and not bother taking control of moving toward the next step in your career.

When my BSF powered my autopilot, I allowed myself to operate on a negative self-fulfilling prophecy that the job I was doing was a waste of time. I would leave home as late as possible, listening to the same BS radio station as I drove to work, smoking the same number of cigarettes, and all the time I was consumed by thoughts of just getting through the day. A day that was then spent clock-watching and avoiding people.

The only thing that punctuated my pointless autopilot existence back then was pipe dreams that I was going to do something about it. I wrote a business plan for a catering company and once bought a website domain name for a clothing company that, deep down, I knew I was never going to do anything with. Those futile dreams just gave more drive to my negative autopilot and my BSF would wake me up the next day to make the same journey to a job I didn't like and do the same tasks whilst waiting for home time.

Looking back, I think I allowed my BSF autopilot to last for over five years. How many people allow it to last for their entire careers?

2. Fear of the unknown

Humans are wired to fear the unknown and the perceived danger that comes with it. Your heart and mind want to predict what will happen next because then we feel safe and secure. A lack of predictability sends you into a spiral of pessimism and your BSF just loves the uncertainty that comes with your fear of the unknown because it wants to tell you what will happen next and make your days feel like a rerun of a rubbish reality TV show.

Not knowing what is going to happen next is one of the most beautiful things on earth. Many of your best moments are spontaneous and the things that you weren't expecting to happen bring you unbridled joy. Yet if your BSF is enjoying itself then you forget all about that and, instead of being curious and open-minded, you convince yourself that you must know exactly how things are going to play out and you ruminate over things that have not even happened yet. I have lost hours and hours to my BSF role playing in my mind telling me how future conversations will be difficult and visualising me cocking things up and people rejecting me just because I don't know for sure what is going to happen. It also paralysed me from making any decisions for years in my earlier career just from having a fear of getting something wrong.

It's why experiences like going on a first date or a job interview, that are meant to be positive encounters which will lead to future happiness and success, see you infected with low self-esteem and nerves that make you want to run as far away as possible even though you WANT to have those experiences and everything that can come with them.

If you've ever been through a redundancy process at work, you will have seen the BSF supercharged by a collective fear of the unknown. The worst part of the redundancy process is immediately after the first announcement is made, when no-one actually knows if they are being made redundant or not. Those days, or sometimes weeks when organisations handle it especially badly, from when the word "redundancies" comes into our lives, are some of the most intense that I have ever experienced.

Once the uncertainty fades and people are told how they are actually affected, the mood changes and, instead of the anticipated despair and frustration, you hear things like *"at least I know now"* or *"redundancy is the best thing that ever happened to me"*. Yet it is very hard to see that the future can be positive when your fear of the unknown empowers your BSF to negatively influence your thoughts and feelings.

'You can't always get what you want
But if you try sometimes,
well, you just might find
You get what you need.'

– THE ROLLING STONES

3. We are all control freaks

We all want to control one thing – ourselves. Feeling like we're not in control of ourselves and what happens to us is like rocket fuel to your BSF. This is because your heart and mind want to be protected from any external threats. When you are at your best and are "in the zone", you feel in control of your emotions and confident that, no matter what happens, you will respond how you want to respond.

Your BSF tricks you into feeling like you're not in control of yourself and reduces your ability to choose a positive response to your thoughts and feelings. This then puts you in a vicious circle, allowing your attitudes and behaviours to become reactive to your BSF. This in turn takes you away from being who you are and doing what you want to do, which leaves you feeling even more out of control. If it's up to your BSF, that vicious circle will continue to intensify as it dials up your desire to be in control of yourself to wanting to control everyone else around you.

Think about that guy in your networking group who doesn't think it's his fault he's moaning. To him he's a victim of a bad manager or a restructure. It's like he's given up his independent thinking and is happy to be a victim of whatever may be going on, giving up his power to respond differently.

It's not the other people on the packed bus that leave you feeling pissed off. It's happened because you want to be in control of getting a seat and ensuring that the journey home is a comfortable one that passes in good time.

You see this desire to be in control at work all the time as people base their feedback on whether or not someone does something in the exact same way or at the same pace that they would have done it. Your BSF shows scant regard for the actual outcome (i.e. was the work done?) or what people actually did (i.e. did they use their initiative?). Instead, it forces you to focus on trying to be in control of everyone and everything, which leaves other people fearing you and tees up your BSF to turn you into a micromanager.

'Do everything you fear
In this there's power
Fear is not to be afraid of.'

– JAMES

4. Your BSF wants to lock you in your comfort zone

One of the biggest unknowns that your BSF fears is that wondrous place that sits outside of your comfort zone. Your comfort zone is that part of your heart and mind where the comfortable, warm room exists with the bean bags and soothing music. If it was up to your BSF, it would kick you into that room, lock the door and throw away the key. We all love a comfort zone because it comes without any threats. We plonk ourselves right on those bean bags and keep doing what we've always done, enjoying that feeling of survival as we sit on our arses in the comfort zone of our BSF.

The comfort zone is a great example of your BSF tricking you into believing that inertia is a good thing. It makes you forget about the rewards that are available when you break out of your comfort zone. It makes you tell yourself that all your hopes and dreams are unobtainable and that the good times are too hard to experience because it takes effort to get your arse off the bean bags and leave the comfort zone.

You see, whilst they are the most powerful and valuable resources on earth, your heart and mind are also a right pair of bastards. Your BSF will love nothing more than you being lazy, telling you that the comfort zone is the place for you to be, encouraging you to forget about having any of the self-motivation and fulfilment that other people get from breaking out of their comfort zone and challenging themselves to be their best version of themselves.

We've all got friends or have worked with people who had talents that could take them way above what they do, but they can't be arsed because their BSF is spinning the keys to their comfort zone around their finger, smiling and reminding them about how much easier it is to walk through the door and grab a bean bag.

"The comfort zone is a great example of your BSF tricking you into believing that inertia is a good thing"

There are plenty of us who set off on a career because we were passionate about something only to find that years later we have forgotten about that passion and have lost interest. Something came along that made that career harder and turned our attention towards the warm glow of the comfort zone where we could bask in our regrets, failed dreams and if onlys.

Christ, if I had stayed in the comfort zones that my BSF tried hard to move me into, I would either be a bored Bank Manager or a stressed-out Operations Director dreading every day and taking it out on people around me with only one goal in life – to keep hold of my job and retire. The mere thought of that fills me with fear, thinking how close I got to allowing my BSF to deny me the chance to do something that I loved with the autonomy and authenticity that I craved.

'I can be who I am
I have no pretence
Only to what you can be
If you want to be
It's a way of living.'

– PAUL WELLER

Those things that fuel your BSF want you to *"stay in your lane"* and *"to take what life gives you"* and all the other cliches that people use to inadvertently keep their BSF hurtling them into negativity and yearning for the good times that they put out of their own reach.

This isn't about climbing Everest or being able to *"live your best life"*. It is about recognising that the BSF taking over your human operating system doesn't lead to anything positive. Instead, we need to realise that we all have the opportunity to do what we want to do, if what we want to do is realistic for us, in the way we want to do it. Even if our way of operating as a human tells us otherwise.

What we need to embrace in us being human is that there are many ways in which our hearts and minds function that work= against us. They sit in the unconsciousness of our lives. Where we truly live is in the consciousness of our lives where we choose how to positively respond to our basic human functioning and break free from the prison of our BSF.

'It's a hard life to live,
so live it well.'

– THE KOOKS

How does your BSF affect you if left unchecked?

1. It keeps you in a negative place and stops you doing what you really want to do. It becomes your cloak and shield of negativity.

2. It keeps you in victim mode. It makes you perceive that BS activities like moaning about the things in your control will protect you from things that are deemed too difficult to do.

3. It skews your perception of yourself, others and situations to the negative, which affects how you feel about yourself and others.

4. It makes your attitudes and behaviours become reactive and restricts you to only ever doing what your thoughts and feelings tell you to do.

'I have this thing where I get older
But never wiser.'

– TAYLOR SWIFT

An example of that last point is the recurring theme that my BSF wrote for me. I would psyche myself up in the morning, telling myself how I was going to do things differently as a leader and how I was going to show all those people around me what I was really capable of and how I didn't have to fit their moulds. I'd do my best Liam Gallagher impersonation belting out "Live Forever" on the way to work, ready to change my experience for the better.

Then I'd get to work and my BSF would kick in and I'd go all shy, insecure and withdrawn and just do all the same things in the same way that I did yesterday, taking out my misery on those around me. When I returned home, I'd moan about it and get up the next day only to do it all over again. It was a perpetual cycle of get up, shower, dream and believe, shit myself (emotionally not physically), bottle it, not be myself, be pissed off, and repeat.

It makes you wonder why you bother getting out of bed some days to put up with the BS coming from your own heart and mind.

Now that I am out of that recurring theme and have done something about my dreams, I am very active on LinkedIn. It's where I build my network and have been successful in getting new clients and work opportunities from my posts and activity on there (in between the bouts of BS comparison triggered by my feed!). I post every day, always with the aim of helping people and showcasing the positive impact that my coaching has on leaders and teams. Yet, my BSF automatically makes me think that anything I share publicly will be met with ridicule and aggressive trolls. It tells me to be reactive and not post anything and get *"back in my place because no-one cares what I have got to say"*. If I allowed my BSF to make me reactive and affect this part of my work, I would be back to singing Oasis songs (although nothing wrong with that, obviously) in preparation for another bad day at work.

'Maybe you're the same as me
We see things they'll never see.'

– OASIS

Everyday examples of reactive attitudes and behaviours of a BSF in operation include: -

- People constantly moaning and doing nothing about the things that they are moaning about.
- A leader slagging off members of their own team.
- Colleagues adopting the *"we'll just do what we've always done"* attitude.
- Leaders avoiding giving feedback.
- Teams blaming other teams for their problems.
- Leaders refusing to listen and telling people to *"just fucking do it"*.

- People demanding attitudes and behaviours from others but refusing to demonstrate those attitudes and behaviours themselves.
- Teams becoming collectively close-minded and judgemental of others.

Reactive attitudes and behaviours become prevalent because it's easy to be reactive. Allowing your BSF to choose your attitude and behaviours is the path of least resistance. It's why many leaders never break their negative habits. It's also why those same dickhead leaders keep getting promoted by the people who react to solving a problem by giving a job to the first dickhead they can find.

When your BSF is operating your attitudes and behaviours, you keep being reactive because you always have an excuse for them:

- *"I have to send loads of e-mails because I'm so busy."*
- *"It's quicker if I do it myself."*
- *"I haven't got time to do leadership coaching because my work is more important."*
- *"My boss told me to do it."*
- *"People should just be grateful that they have a job."*
- *"That's just the way it is here."*

They are just some of the reactive excuses I have heard from people whose attitudes and behaviours are clearly contaminated with their BSF.

A great example of your BSF in action that most can relate to is how it tells you to look for the worst even in good situations. Take positive feedback as a case in point. Even when someone is telling you that you did a good job, your BSF tells you to look for the things you did wrong or the bad part of what you have done. I see this with participants of Enthuse leadership development programmes who will get good feedback from myself and their peers and their response will be to ask *"What do I need to do differently?"* or *"What is your negative feedback?"* Your BSF loves sabotaging your attitudes and behaviours even when things have gone really well. On more than one occasion, I have said to coaching clients, *"It's OK that sometimes you nail it. Just accept the positive feedback and don't let your BSF ruin it for you."* Your BSF is always lurking in the background, trying to escape from its dark cave of doom to ruin even your good days.

You might recognise some of those examples in you, your team or your organisation. A favourite reactive BSF behaviour for me as a manager was to jump on my team when they made a mistake or when someone else flagged something. I would be very direct with people and simply repeat targets and ways of working without listening, reducing some people to tears with my insistence on them doing things perfectly. My excuse for this would be *"they should know better"* and I would use that as my attack and defence, leaving a trail of ruined relationships and my own damaged reputation behind me. All of that was in the name of keeping my BSF happy!

'Your brain can be your truest friend, or it can be your mortal enemy.'

LOUIS THEROUX

Why we need to shut down our BSF

- So you can feel comfortable and more confident in your own skin. You must shut down your BSF so you can choose to do the things that bring you joy at work and that positively challenge you.
- So you can stop being led by negative thoughts and feelings.
- So you can get over your limiting beliefs about yourself that are holding you back.
- So you can go home and be the husband, wife, dad, mum, son, daughter, brother, sister and friend that you want to be.

- ➡ So you can make the positive choices that you want to make.
- ➡ So you can be who you want to be and have the experiences you want to have.
- ➡ So you can be confident in yourself and be self-motivated.
- ➡ So you can have the impact you want to have on others and build the relationships that make you want to go to work every day.

Operating from your BSF doesn't feel nice or lead to good days. It's debilitating for your confidence and ruins your reputation. It infiltrates your relationships and turns them toxic, meaning being who you really are and having your desired impact becomes an impossible task. It produces ego and bravado to mask how you really think and feel and makes you come across like a right dick.

Whilst I have met many people who have demonstrated all of the above, me included, during my darkest times with my BSF, I have never met anyone who says that's what they WANT from their life and work. I have worked with hundreds of leaders and teams where I ask them the question *"how do you want to come across to other people?"* and never has anyone responded with *"I want to come across like a right dick"*. Yet, we all know a few people who do come across in just that way!

'In a world so torn
Where is inspiration?
Whole world in a storm
There must be something better.'

– PAUL WELLER

When you put in the time to shut down your BSF, you become much more proactive and quicken your ability to respond to your negative thoughts and feelings in the moment. It's still going to tell you that you're not good enough and make you feel inferior. Shutting down your BSF means you can rapidly acknowledge it for what it is, BS, and move on. This will mean that you no longer get caught up in your own thoughts and feelings and you stop judging yourself or others for having those thoughts and feelings. It also enables you to stop reacting in a negative way so that you are able to take a breath and consider what you want to happen in any situation.

At the start of the work I do with leaders and teams, it is commonplace for a lot of conversations to evolve around the things that they can't do or that they want to do and don't have enough time. This usually centres around things like reflection time, having fewer meetings and calls, finding the time to talk through their challenges with peers, reading a book, doing things differently and spending more time delegating to and developing their teams. What's stopping them is nothing to do with time or capability, it is because their BSF has paralysed their ability to make positive choices.

'Always make your choices for the right reasons.'

Putting time into you, and choosing to focus on the good things you do, leads to better days and gives you the experiences you want from your life and work. When my BSF was running my heart and mind, I felt like I was carrying around my own grey, rain cloud. Now that I have chosen to shut it down, I feel like my days are filled with sunshine (and I live in the North West of England!). Sure, that might sound like a cliche or some BS in itself, but I am speaking from experience here; shutting down your BSF feels much better than leaving it to run (and ruin) your life for you.

Your BSF is like living in a never-ending sliding doors moment where your happiness and success rests on every decision being made by your BSF or by you. Here are some examples of how your BSF puts you on the knife edge of despair or hope: -

Decision made by your BSF	**Decision made by you**
➡ Don't apply for the job you want.	➡ Apply for the job you want.
➡ Cancel your team's 1-2-1's.	➡ Engage in frequent, good conversations with your team.
➡ Avoid doing the things you love doing.	➡ Do the things you love doing.
➡ Doom scroll on social media.	➡ Only use the social media platform/s of your choice and literally speak to and spend time with the people that you are actually "friends" with or want to be "connected" to.
➡ Moan about insignificant BS.	➡ Ignore insignificant BS.
➡ Watch shite TV that you're not really interested in.	➡ Read a book. Or get some kip.
➡ Avoid giving and asking for feedback.	➡ Have regular feedback conversations that build trust and supercharge your confidence.
➡ Keep working for a dickhead boss.	➡ Leave your dickhead boss and work somewhere that deserves you.

The above examples are very basic yet speak for themselves in terms of which decisions we would all prefer to be able to make. The outcomes from the decisions made by you are always much more positive and always give you the chance to feel invigorated by doing something of your own volition and what you will learn from it. When your BSF decision fails, you feel like a boxer who has been battered and can't get back up off the canvas. Whereas your own decisions made by your own positive choices, even if they "fail", mean you can get back up and keep fighting.

Your BSF triggers the negativity that drives your bad decisions. When you shut it down, you take back control and make the good decisions you want to make for yourself. I am only on page twenty-three of Google Docs as I write this book and already my BSF has told me that I can't be arsed to write it, it will be shit, no-one will read it anyway and I should just go to the pub instead.

Whilst the pub always sounds appealing to me (although it's currently 10:39am on a Tuesday!), I don't choose those thoughts and feelings. What I can choose is how to positively respond and crack on with writing the book because it is what I really want to do and I believe that it will help the right people.

'Awaken all the ghosts in your mind
Speak of all the good that you find
Live and learn that life is not unkind
Understand the demons that you fight.'

– PAUL WELLER

Even the organic benefits that come from shutting down your BSF make this the most worthwhile thing you will do with your time and energy. You see, a byproduct of shutting down your BSF is that you become an expert on the most powerful tool that you have at your disposal – YOU.

And by becoming an expert on you, you will develop and apply the greatest power you have as a human being, which is to choose a positive response to your thoughts and feelings. That is the power that you unleash by shutting down your BSF. Your thoughts and feelings will do whatever they want, especially when coming from your BSF. That isn't the bit of you that needs to change – you need to change (and will change) how you respond to your thoughts and feelings.

Imagine a day where you will still have some negative thoughts and feelings yet, instead of ruining your day, you choose a positive response and still work with confidence and self-belief, allowing yourself to have a good day even though some of your thoughts and feelings are bad. This isn't about ignoring or using the worn-out "*swan*" analogy of no-one seeing you paddling for your life. This is about real things that you can do that will turn reality into something positive for you.

Even the days when you wake up with your BSF telling you to anticipate bad things happening and that dark clouds are forming, you can stand up to it, tell it to fuck right off and go and have the type of days that leave you feeling as happy as Geena Davis was after she shagged Brad Pitt in *Thelma & Louise*.

'Louise, no matter what happens,
I'm glad I came with you.'

– THELMA FROM "THELMA & LOUISE"

The practical daily techniques that you use to shut down your BSF will make your life more positive and you more confident. You don't need to remember any acronyms or recite what someone else tells you to do. Because your BSF is so simple, I am going to keep it simple to shut it down with nothing convoluted or complicated. This will keep the pressure off you, as you won't have to remember any scientific theories or models (I've researched them for you), and enable you to harness the special powers that you have as the emotional creature that you are. I have got your back; shutting down your BSF is something we do together. I have done the hard graft, studying neuroscience and emotional intelligence (my certificates are in my loft somewhere if you want to see them!), and I will bring it to life for you here in a way that is easy to remember, relate to and use every day.

We all want a calmer, more rewarding and fulfilled life and, whatever that means to you, shutting down your BSF will unlock it for you as you keep it simple so that it can give you what you want. At its heart, what we'll be doing is recognising the thoughts and feelings that trigger negative experiences and learn how to create positive ones for ourselves instead.

Many people exist in a world of perpetual negativity led by their BSF, which only gets punctuated by a perceived positive break at the weekends. How many millions of people around the world do you think live like this every week?

- They spend Sunday evening worrying about work and the week ahead.
- They go to work dreading Monday.

- They get past Wednesday and tell themselves *"the weekend is nearly here"*.
- They then celebrate Friday and the weekend for no other reason than *"it's better than being in work"*.
- They start all over again come Sunday evening.

Your BSF keeps you in this cycle by making you think it's OK because you get to another Friday at the end of every week. It tells you that a highlight of your week is making it past another "hump day". Newsflash – there is a Wednesday every single fucking week of your life! I know, I have lived like that and, believe me, it is not a good existence. For me, this led to nothing but boredom, frustration, weekday hangovers and regret.

Your BSF is great at dangling a carrot which offers the same banal reward that keeps you on the hamster wheel of misery. You are not going to be one of those people running on the revolving wheel covered in hamster shit because shutting down your BSF is going to show you that there is a better way. It will be a kinder way, a more supportive way and a way that enables you to be your best version of yourself on your own terms.

'Wake up, it's a beautiful morning
(wake up)
The sun shining for your eyes
Wake up, it's so beautiful (wake up).'

– THE BOO RADLEYS

A final note: your BSF does not want you to shut it down, and it will play dirty...

Your BSF will tell you that it is too hard to shut down or that a different book that you haven't yet read will have all the answers. It wants you to get lost in all the psychobabble because it will always know more about that than you ever will. It wants you to tell yourself that you have to be an expert in psychology to choose a positive response to the nonsense thoughts and feelings that it produces because that makes you doubt yourself even more. And I don't think I need to remind you that any resistance that your BSF comes up with is... well... BS!

It isn't easy to shut down your BSF because you have to challenge your own thoughts and feelings. It's hard enough to be aware of it, never mind change how we respond to it. The hardest thing to do is challenge our own thoughts and feelings because we believe them all to be true. It's much easier to challenge others when we disagree with them, yet we find it so hard to challenge our own thoughts and feelings because they come from within us – surely they must be right!!

When those thoughts and feelings have been a pattern that we've been following for many years, they create the moulds we fit into. Your BSF fights really hard and really dirty to stop you from breaking the mould that it sets for you.

Your BSF is very good at convincing you that it speaks gospel truth, like when it was telling me that I absolutely bombed on that stage in London and should have just legged it off stage after I fell over. I could hear nothing else other than my BSF, yet no-one else in the room was sharing its opinions. That is just one mould that I have had to break free from to stop my BSF from taking over my life.

'It was the light of a candle,
in the depths of the dark
And there was a fire,
it danced in your eyes
A beautiful world and a beautiful mind
You've got a beautiful mind.'

– WUNDERHORSE

What have we done in this chapter

- Introduced you to your BSF and the impact it has on you
- Called out some of the BS that comes from our BSF
- Reminded ourselves that we are human which fuels our BSF
- Explained the BSF production cycle and why we each have a BSF
- Shown how the BSF affects you and the importance of shutting it down

Coaching questions to get you thinking about your BSF...

- When can you recognise your BSF firing up?
- What bullshit exists in your world?
- What powers your BSF?
- How does your BSF affect you?
- Where does it most affect you?
- Why do you want to shut down your BSF?
- How will you feel when you have shut down your BSF?

CHAPTER TWO

A REAL-LIFE BULLSHIT FACTORY IN ACTION

In this chapter you'll witness the full force of a BSF in action. You're about to read a real-life story. This actually happened to me. There is a very good chance that this is the part of the book that will leave the biggest mark on you and the bit that you will remember and tell others about. That is because you might have experienced something (or someone!) like it too. This chapter lays bare how the BSF can take over people and negatively influence their days. You will find some of it incredulous and baulk at the absurdity, but that, ladies and gentlemen, is the BSF at its magnificent worst. It takes people into seemingly "normal" situations and turns them into something that no-one wants to get out of bed for.

'When I counted up my demons
I saw there was one for every day.'

– COLDPLAY

It was a beautiful sunny day in West Yorkshire. Driving through England's green and pleasant land to get to where I was working that day made me feel so lucky to be doing what I do. It made me even more excited for the day ahead, where I was working with a group for the first time to kick off their leadership development programme.

Close your eyes and imagine the most picturesque scene of the English countryside in the sunshine and you might get somewhere close to where I was that morning.

I arrived at my destination, which was a beautiful modern office built into a hillside, and saw a visitor's car parking space with my name on it and thought to myself *how good is this*?! The first thing I did when I got out of my car was take a picture of my name in a frame marking my parking space and then took a selfie with the beautiful green hills draped in sunshine in the background. I sent both pictures to my wife, telling her that I was about to have an amazing day.

All the arrangements had been made beforehand for me to arrive at 8am for a 9:30 start and I had all the contact and room details to ask for. I had completed all of my preparation, all the communications with the client (who for the purposes of this story, we'll call Computers Ltd) leading up to today had been positive; I felt really confident about the day ahead. It was the kind of day I live for and, as a bonafide morning person, I was flying and couldn't wait to get in there, get my tunes on and get everything set up for the participants. I headed into the building with a big smile on my face, taking in all of the wonderful surroundings.

'Is this the life that we're just living in?'

– THE WAR ON DRUGS

I was met at reception by a lovely security guard who welcomed me and showed me where to sign in. He also politely explained that he couldn't let me into the room as "day visitors" had to be registered by the receptionist who would arrive shortly and show me to the training room that I was booked in. I was invited to take a seat on some comfy sofas whilst I waited and was also shown where the visitor toilets were and where I could help myself to a hot drink whilst I waited.

I asked him if there was a parcel behind reception marked for my attention, or for "Peter in L&D", as the training materials had been sent via courier for my arrival. He looked and said he couldn't see anything, but when the receptionist arrived, they would be able to check in the post room for me (as it was locked). He assured me they would know where it was and would help me once they arrived. His politeness and the way he engaged with me gave me confidence that there would be no problems.

This just gets better I thought to myself as I thanked the security guard and made my way to the sofas. As I sat there, I took in the splendour of the office. This wasn't your typical reception waiting area. It was part of a huge foyer which was illuminated by the morning sun through the glass frontage of the building. In the centre was a huge open staircase that led up to the floors above and was currently full of people arriving for work who all seemed chirpy enough and were greeting each other on their way up and down the stairs.

I sat there waiting for around five minutes, totally transfixed by the arrival of more and more people and feeling happy to just wait as I had plenty of time and had been made to feel welcome. I also noticed a set of double doors opposite with a sign above saying "All meeting rooms this way", which made me feel confident that the room I was going to be in for the day was not too far away from where I was waiting.

"She's here now, mate," said the security guard to me as he came from behind the reception desk to make his exit from the night shift.

"OK, cool, thanks for your help. Have a great day," I replied, also giving him a thumbs up just to seal my gratitude for how welcoming he'd been.

I looked towards the receptionist who was getting settled behind her desk, turning her computer on and all the other stuff that people do when they arrive at work. I didn't want to impose myself on her so I patiently sat back down for a couple of minutes so she could be ready to help me.

'Have you ever watched the day,
passing by your door
Powerless to change its course,
your feet fixed to the floor
When all the people you thought you
knew are changing more and more.'

– THE STYLE COUNCIL

I decided to go over and introduce myself as she looked ready at her desk, so I walked over with a polite smile on my face.

"Morning. How are you? I'm Tim Roberts. I'm running the leadership course here today."

No verbal response came from the receptionist, just a side-eye glance in my direction which made me feel a bit nervous. I hate it when people don't reply when you speak to them.

I tried again. *"Erm, I think we're in meeting room one. It's been organised via Peter in L&D and the security guard said you'd be able to let me in so I can get set up for when people start to arrive,"* I said, hoping that me giving more information would encourage her to engage in a conversation with me.

"I don't start until half-eight," came her reply without even looking at me.

So many things raced through my mind as my happiness and excitement for the day ahead was being slowly depleted by my interaction with the receptionist. I decided to play her at her own game and respond to what she had said. I looked at the digital wall clock behind her which read 08:19 and I thought *I can wait another 11 minutes.*

"Oh right, sorry. So, if I come back at half-eight, will you be able to let me in the meeting room and get everything set up?"

"Yes, as long as I know which one it is as we'll have other courses running today."

"OK no probs. I've got all the details from Peter, so I'll be able to let you know which room I am in." I had literally just told her that we're in meeting room one!

Silence again as she typed away on her keyboard instead of acknowledging what I had just said. I walked away slowly in the hope that she would say something to me as I walked away but nothing came and I retreated back to the comfy sofas and decided to use the time to read through my notes and do what prep I could do before I was able to get into the room. I hoped to use the time sat there waiting for 8:30 to arrive to allow the receptionist to turn into a human being who had the ability and desire to talk to people as part of her job.

'Bright kid, leaves school
Gets job, hates it
Fakes it, too long
Sees no, way out.'

– SAM FENDER

A few minutes later, I saw someone approach the reception desk and thought to myself *"oh my god, don't wind her up!!"* and I couldn't help but take my attention away from my prep and observe what happened next. The interchange between receptionist and employee went something like this: -

"Hello. I am coming back from maternity leave today and don't have one of the new passes so my boss said to ask for a temporary pass and he would then approve and order my new pass for me today," said the employee with a smile on her face.

The receptionist slowly lifted her head from her screen. *"Has your boss ordered you a temporary pass?"* she asked without any inquiry to how the person felt returning from maternity leave or asking about how her baby was; you know, like most pleasant people would do seeing as the employee was clearly a little apprehensive about being back to work for the first time that morning.

"Err, I don't know. They told me last week that I could come to reception and give my details to get a temporary pass so I can get into the office today and then my new pass would come from HR later today when I have my picture taken for it." The returning employee now visibly looked worried and unsure of what was going on.

Just give her the fucking pass, nobhead, I thought to myself.

"All temporary passes have to be approved," came the curt reply from the receptionist followed by silence as she again diverted her eye contact from the person she was speaking to.

"OK. How does my boss do that for me?" asked the employee, now turning from nervous to frustrated.

"They have to e-mail reception and then it would be on the desk to be picked up," explained the receptionist, now sitting back in her chair, arms folded and staring at the employee as if to say *"thou shalt not pass"* through her body language alone.

"Could you please check if you have the e-mail and the pass as my boss told me he had already sorted it?" was the employee's reply, now going back at the receptionist much more quickly.

"I don't start until half-eight," came the predictable response, which I was now starting to think must be her favourite catchphrase. *"You'll have to wait over there because I can't let anyone through without a pass,"* she said, motioning to where I was sitting.

The employee sighed and decided that her best chance of being able to get into the place where she worked was to not bother with the receptionist and decided to join me on the comfy sofas and ring her boss. She made the call and within a couple of minutes a man, who I am presuming to be her boss, arrived at the bottom of the stairs and told her to come over and he would let her in with his pass. And off they went up the stairs to get on with their day.

Well played, I thought in relation to the employee's response and her boss for helping her out. It made me sit back and think about what I had just witnessed. I wondered if the receptionist's reputation preceded her so that the returning employee's boss knew it was better to break the rules and take her in with his pass rather than try to obtain the temporary one that I didn't doubt he had requested prior to today. It was probably already sitting somewhere on the receptionist's desk waiting for the returning employee to collect it!

'Why don't you do what's right instead of doing what's wrong?'

– THE RECORD COMPANY

It was now 08:28 on the clock behind reception and my parents' head kicked in telling me to go to the toilet before I made a second attempt to get the receptionist to help me as I then expected I would need to prep the room in double time before people started to arrive. I walked towards where the security guard had told me the visitors' toilet was, making sure not to look at the receptionist.

"Where are you going?" I heard as I reached the door.

I stopped in my tracks and turned to the receptionist, who had suddenly found her voice, *"I am going to the visitors' toilet. The security guard told me it's OK to use it."* Again, no response, she just turned away from me, which I took as her approval for me to go to the toilet. I pressed on to the toilet with all sorts going through my mind, mainly trying to work out how my day had gone from getting off to such a great start to now feeling like I was facing a battle to be able to do my job thanks to the cantankerous receptionist.

As I walked back to the reception area, I noticed the post room next to the toilets and outside it was a box with my name on it. I looked closer and realised this was the training materials that I had enquired after with the security guard and picked it up, thinking at least I didn't have to ask the receptionist to help me find it. I walked back out into the reception area with the box only to be accosted straight away.

"What do you think you're doing with that box?" was the predictable, aggressive question sent my way from you-know-who.

"It's the training materials that I'll be using for today. They got delivered last week and I just saw the box with my name on it outside the post room so I collected it ready for getting in the room and setting up." That last bit was added in a vain attempt to remind her that I needed her to let me into said meeting room. I kept on walking past her thinking that my explanation was sufficient enough for any human being to accept. Not for this one though!

"You can't just take random boxes. They have to be signed for. You'll have to put it back." She actually stood up now, pointing after me.

I stopped and my shoulders dropped. I thought about just ignoring the bitch but, as I still needed her to let me in the meeting room, I returned to face her and did my best to politely explain that I was not going to put the box back.

"Sorry, I should have let you know that I had seen the box and asked if I could take it. It is clearly marked for my attention." I tilted the box to show that it was indeed addressed FAO Tim Roberts (care of "Peter in L&D"). *"I just thought it would be easier for me to grab it now rather than trouble you to get it for me as I am going to use it today for the course I am running."*

"I don't know who you are, so how do I know that box is for you?" she replied, which was possibly one of the most ridiculous things I have ever had said to me. It's training materials in a cardboard box not the fucking crown jewels!

"I introduced myself before. I'm Tim Roberts. I have signed in and am happy to show you some ID. You could also call 'Peter in L&D' and he'll confirm that it is OK for me to take the box." I wasn't giving it back now and placed it next to the comfy sofa and sat back down feeling exhausted and wondering what the actual fuck was going on. Then I saw that the time was now 08:35 and thought my best chance was to get into the meeting room and away from the receptionist from hell. I marched back up to her desk and kept my dignity by smiling and being really polite as I asked, *"Would you please be able to let me into the meeting room now? I am just conscious that people will be arriving soon and they won't know where to go."* I tried my best to appeal to her good side (if she even had one) and subtly tried to suggest that if you don't let me in the room then you'll have 12 people bothering you and loitering around reception.

This now brings us to my favourite part of this whole interaction. She turned to look at the clock on the wall, seeking confirmation that it had passed 08:30 and then turned back to me and said, *"I just need to go and do something. You'll have to wait there."* With that, she stood, grabbed her handbag, walked from behind the reception desk and through the pass-activated barriers that I could not get through and disappeared behind some double doors into the office area.

'Sometimes, I wonder why we bother at all.'

– DMA'S

I decided to stand my ground and wait for her at the reception desk. She did return quite quickly, which made me wonder where she'd been in such a rush to go. And then I saw it in her hands... She'd been to buy a packet of crisps. A fucking packet of crisps!! We all need to eat but imagine having the attitude that buying a packet of crisps (at 08:35!) is more important than helping out a visitor who has been nothing but polite and patient with you. The same visitor whom it is your job to make feel welcome.

You can shove your crisps up your arse, I thought, in a state of incredulity at the resistance she was putting up to just helping me out and getting me out of her way. I decided not to show my frustration and to stay positive because experience has taught me that when dealing with someone this grumpy, the best thing you can do is be overly polite and cheerful with them.

I gave her a little smile as she carefully put her crisps in her desk drawer and I again enquired if she could please let me into the meeting room that was booked for me. I even addressed her as if this was the first time I had asked. Once again, avoiding eye contact (I think that is her superpower), this time, she actually started to help me and opened up a diary marked "meeting rooms" with written entries for today's date.

"What is your name and what are you here for?" she asked without any hint of sarcasm or humour as if I hadn't already told her... twice!

'It's not OK to be this way.'

– THE ENEMY

"I'm Tim Roberts and I am facilitating the leadership programme. The room will be booked under 'Peter from L&D' who told me it was meeting room one." At this point, I was willing to play her game just to get away from the curmudgeon.

"Peter has booked meeting room one for today and your name is also in here. It says it doesn't start until 9:30," she stated in a way as if to suggest I wasn't going to be allowed in there for another 45 minutes. I decided to ignore that.

"That's great. Is it through there? I'll go through and get everything set up," I asked, pointing to the doors signposted "All meeting rooms this way". I even tried to start shifting away from her, thinking this was my chance to escape now she had acknowledged what room I was in. How naive was I? Of course, this crank had another way of stopping me getting on with the job I was here to do for the company that she worked for.

"Do you work for Computers Ltd?" was her retort.

"No, I am a consultant who partners with your L&D Team. This is my first time here, but we've got another five days after today, so I'll be back here quite a bit in the next six months."

Why did I just tell her that? I thought, facing up to the fact that I might have to put up with all her bullshit every time I come back.

"I can't let you in unless there is someone who works for us with you. No visitors are allowed in the meeting rooms on their own," she said with a triumphant air to her very matter-of-fact answer.

"OK, what am I supposed to do in the meantime?" I asked, hoping that asking her an open question might get a more open answer.

"You'll have to wait until someone who works here turns up and they can go into the room with you."

I had to think quickly here because I knew that none of my contacts were based at this site, and I didn't yet know anyone who would be attending the course. I didn't want to give her any more ammunition to ruin my morning and decided that being even more patient was best for my own sanity.

"Can one of the participants go into the room with me when they arrive?" I suggested, feeling quite proud of myself having come up with that idea.

"Do they work for us?"

You can probably imagine the kind of things that entered my head in terms of how I wanted to reply to what was possibly the stupidest question she'd asked me yet.

"Yes, everyone attending works for Computers Ltd," I explained, trying to put a positive tone of voice on whilst sighing inside my mind.

"Yes. As long as they are based here or have an ID pass, they can let you in the room." I was happy to settle for this and thanked her and said I would wait until someone arrived, asking her if she would please let me know when someone arrives for the course. To which she replied, absolutely deadpan, with *"I don't know who they are."*

At this point, I wanted to scream in her face *"THEY WILL INTRODUCE THEMSELVES TO YOU AND ASK WHAT MEETING ROOM THEIR COURSE IS IN, YOU FUCKING IDIOT!!!!"*

However, I decided not to give her the satisfaction of me getting wound up and simply said, *"OK, cool,"* and walked back to the comfy sofa and plotted my next move.

I decided to look at the list of participant names that I had been sent before today and then listen out for one of them going to the reception desk, watching out for anyone going through the double doors to the promised land of "all meeting rooms" beyond. I also chose to use the time to work through in my mind what was the least bit of prep I needed to do to get the day started in case I didn't get into the room until 9:30. I took some deep breaths and reminded myself that it was not the end of the world and that the receptionist's attitude only reflected on her, not me.

'Good morning day, how do you do
I wonder – what will you do for me?
I should be on my way, I should be earning pay,
I should be all the things that I'm not.'

– THE STYLE COUNCIL

Five minutes or so later, I saw a young woman arrive and look around the reception area like she wasn't familiar with this office. I watched as she saw the "all meeting rooms" doors and she headed through them. I stood up like an excited dog does when their owner returns home, thinking this could be my moment. I put my notes away and started to pick up my bag and the box of training materials and was planning on streaming past the receptionist to follow my hero into the meeting room.

I didn't even get to take one stride away from the sofa before the young woman came back out of the double doors, again looking a little lost. She spotted the receptionist and started walking towards her. At this moment, I felt like I was in one of those horror movies where someone is going to enter the room where the murderer is hiding and you shout at the screen telling them not to go in there because you know a terrible fate awaits them.

I decided I had to let the innocent young woman put herself in danger and I watched on, wincing from what was about to happen. I really wanted to save her but knew I had to let it play out as my best hope of finally getting into meeting room one.

"Hiya, I am Charlotte from our Leeds site. I am on a leadership training course here today. Do you know what room we're in?" asked the young woman of my miserable mate,

the receptionist. I felt like I was watching a lamb about to be slaughtered and quickly looked at my participant list to see if there was a Charlotte on there. Bingo! She was on the list and I felt like a long-lost friend had just turned up. Then my euphoria was punctuated by the devil in the form of a receptionist.

"What course is it?" is the response she offers, still not making eye contact of course.

Take a wild guess, you ignorant bitch!! My heart sank as I thought this and I am still taken aback by the pure ignorance of this woman.

"It's the management development programme. We're starting it today, but I can't remember what room the invite said on it. I have been on a few courses here before and they're usually in meeting room one but today is the first day of the programme so I'm not sure if we'll be in a different room," says Charlotte brightly, probably expecting a normal response from someone whose job it is to welcome visitors and help them find where they need to go. But oh no, not here...

"No-one has told me about any courses today," comes yet another unhelpful statement from the receptionist.

"What? Apart from the bloke who has been waiting for nearly an hour and is standing less than five metres away from you? Not the bloke who asked only five minutes ago

for you to let him know when someone arrives for the course that he has told you that he is facilitating here today? You ginormous dickhead!" is what I wanted to leap up and say, but I decided to make the right impression with Charlotte rather than attack the receptionist.

I walked swiftly over with a smile on my face, ignoring Neggy Nelly behind the desk and introducing myself to Charlotte. I reassured her that I was running the course and asked her to show her ID pass to the receptionist and then we could both go into meeting room one.

Charlotte was pleased to see me and presented her ID pass, which finally gained us the nod to go into meeting room one. It was sanctioned by the receptionist, making a noise which was half grunt, half sigh and genuinely sounded like she farted out of her mouth.

I'll take a mouth fart if it gets me away from you, I think as I quickly grab my bag and the box of training materials and head over towards the sanctuary of meeting room one having the obligatory small talk with Charlotte. We head through the double doors and find meeting room one in front of us. Charlotte offers to open the doors whilst I carry the training materials box and my bag but when she tries to, we discover that meeting room one is in fact locked! At this point, I raise my head to the sky and say, *"Of course it is locked,"* whilst half sighing, half laughing.

Charlotte reads my signals and asks how long I had been waiting to get into the room, and I know that she can sense that I've had a rough ride with the guard dog of a receptionist. I let her know that I had been there for an hour and chose to remain professional by not slagging off the company that she worked for or the receptionist herself. Instead, I suggested that we head back to get the key, asking Charlotte to accompany me as I expected that she would be the only one of us allowed to take it (and also for my personal safety, but I didn't tell her that). We left our bags and the box at the door to meeting room one and returned to enemy territory.

'And all of my anger
You take on the chin
And I get you down
I get you down.'

– SAM FENDER

Charlotte and I walked back to the receptionist and I decided to be brave and take on the responsibility of tackling the latest barrier that I faced that morning. I say with very soft intonation and a polite look on my face, *"Meeting room one is locked."* Before I can add any question about where we can get the key from, I am interrupted by the receptionist who appeared to see this as her perfect opportunity to put the icing on the cake.

"You need a key," she said completely dead-pan and with zero offer of where to get said key from.

No shit, Sherlock. If only someone had told me earlier in my life that in order to open a locked door you need a key!! is what I was thinking and I was also pretty sure that Charlotte was now thinking the same thing and appeared embarrassed by the behaviour of one of her colleagues as we looked at each other, seemingly searching to be anywhere but there.

I take a breath and ask, *"Where can we get the key from?"*

"I've got it here..."

Yes, she did genuinely just let us walk off to meeting room one knowing that it was locked but without telling us that we needed a key, a key that she knew she had. All of that despite me having waited there for an hour to get into said meeting room one. You literally couldn't make this shit up!!

"But I can't..." continued the receptionist. It is at this point that I do one of the bravest things of my entire life and dare to interrupt her.

"You can't give it to me, yes, because I don't work for Computers Ltd? Is it OK to give it to Charlotte please, who does work for Computers Ltd?" comes my intervention.

To my amazement, she rose from her seat and opened up a box marked "meeting room keys" and asked for Charlotte's signature before she handed the key over to her. Charlotte immediately handed it to me as if to make a point and show how ridiculous this whole situation is. I felt like I had just been given the freedom of the city and thanked Charlotte before we both turned to walk away.

"Where have you both parked?" came the question that followed us in a narky tone of voice. It really felt like she just wanted to have the last word.

"In the red bays marked for visitors from other sites," Charlotte told her, adding, *"I always park there and booked it online when I booked the course."* The tyrant on reception accepted this and I thought *go, Charlotte!* before I became her target.

"What about you? Where have you parked?" she asked, with an accentuation on the *"you"* suggesting I was the dog shit that she had just scraped from the sole of her shoe.

I took a step away from the reception desk, breathed and prepared my response like I was about to sink the winning putt in the Ryder Cup, hit the winning runs in an Ashes test and score the winning goal in the World Cup final all in one. I declared with real gusto and a sense of *"fuck you"*, even slightly raising my voice with a smile on my face to deliver *"In the space with my name on it. Thanks for all your help, have a great day,"* before walking off into the sunset of meeting room one.

'Who's been fooling my emotions?
'There's nothing you can say,
even if you're game enough
'Cause I've been holding on for so long
Honey, won't you say maybe we can
change it up?'

– DMA'S

What does the tale of the irascible receptionist show us?

I wanted to introduce you to my receptionist fiend to show you how a Bullshit Factory impacts on people and those around them. It is in the real world and I am sure you have your own "receptionist" story that you can relate to. Or perhaps *you* are the "receptionist"?!

There is no way that the receptionist (I have to keep calling her "receptionist" as, unsurprisingly, she never told me her name!) got up that morning and consciously told herself that what she wanted to do that day was piss people off, appear really miserable, refuse to help people and to make herself look ridiculous by prioritising a packet of crisps over someone who needed her help.

Of course, she didn't.

I know it's hard to believe, and we have all encountered, or continue to encounter, someone like that, but no-one consciously chooses to be that way. I am sure that deep (deep, deep, deep!) down, my receptionist mate from West Yorkshire is really a lovely person. What happened to her, like so many other people, is she allowed her BSF to take over, making her behave in a way that makes other people feel like every interaction with her is a battle and like they have to be overly positive just to make a point. It must have built up over time because there is no way she could have been like that at her interview and still got the job!

There are three key things that my interaction with the irascible receptionist shows us...

1. Real, awful attitudes and behaviours that result from your BSF

It features four people who all got up and went to work that morning in a beautiful setting. Yet, because of one person's

BSF, four people had a negative experience which is not what they got out of bed for.

I am including the receptionist in the "four people" as she definitely did not come across like she was living her best life that day! It's a great example of how one person's BSF can create a ripple effect, ruining other people's days and generating a toxic cloud over people at their place of work. The receptionist at that office was literally the face of the organisation *"welcoming"* all visitors to their Head Office.

This is why I have used the reprehensible receptionist to bring the BSF to life. Her attitudes and behaviours were so overtly negative that they were nuclear. My exchange with her perfectly captures what happens to people when their BSF controls them and convinces them that reactive attitudes and behaviours are the right way to interact with other people.

'One of these days I'm gonna give myself a real good talking to.'

– JIMI GOODWIN

2. An individual BSF has a butterfly effect on the rest of the organisation

People must have dreaded dealing with the receptionist at "Computers Ltd". Not one single person who entered the building whilst I was waiting that morning said *"good morning"* to her and she never once lifted her head up from her keyboard (or her salt and vinegar crisps!) as tens of people streamed past her on their way into work that bright, sunny day. Imagine being her boss and how that would feel every day, possibly having to give her feedback on her attitude. Think about her poor team (if she was allowed to be part of a team, that is). Can you even contemplate going into a meeting with her or trying to get her to buy in to a new idea or support you with a piece of work? I'm shitting myself just thinking about it, and I've actually met her!

I have described the impact she had on me, and I was just a visitor there for the day. What if you were going for a job interview there and were already nervous before you had to contend with her and ask her to let your interviewer know that you had arrived?

One BSF, like our receptionist's, can destroy how it feels in a place of work. It sets the tone for others and tells people that it is OK to be rude and treat colleagues and visitors like crap. I have genuinely worked for and with organisations where people might as well have *"I'll do what I've always done"* tattooed on their forehead whilst moaning to anyone who will listen about how bad it is to work there. Let's not forget the *"that's just the way it is here"* brigade, whose BSF drains the living daylights out of people.

The BSF goes around the whole organisation in all directions. Why would a CEO spend their career "getting to the top" to then treat people like numbers and behave like a narcissist? What about all those newly promoted managers who are filled with joie de vivre when they start their new job only to then turn into the mood hoovers a few years later? People fit snugly into the BSF way of life instead of having enthusiasm for where they spend most of their time. They end up telling you that they dislike positive people as if it is something to be proud of. I'd love to know what the cost to organisations is, in terms of money and productivity, as a result of work environments being invaded by a BSF army.

I will leave it to your imagination as to what I have said to people about "Computers Ltd" since I met her, and whether or not you think I pitch it as a good place to work.

'And I can't be certain that they're
Pulling the curtain on me
And if tomorrow's a burden
Then I'm still learning to be.'

– DMA'S

3. Why culture change in organisations is so hard to achieve

The BSF rails against things like company culture because it is a threat. Your BSF wants to set a negative culture for you to work in and wants to shield you against the optimism of building a better place to work. The BSF tells us it's all a waste of time with forced fun and free fruit (some of the shit versions in reality are all forced fun and free fruit!!), which is categorised as being "pink and fluffy" and "that's HR's job" by your BSF to keep it at a safe distance because God forbid you'd actually try to enjoy your work and positively engage with the other humans who work there! So many people are sick of their shitty place of work, but the BSF that drives it all gets stronger and stronger as any positive attempts to change it get rejected.

Put yourself in the shoes of the People Team at "Computers Ltd". You have worked hard on identifying where change is needed and created a strategy to implement the change to help people get more out of working there. As part of the plan, you run some workshops that everyone is invited to and the receptionist is joining the one that you're running today. She would definitely be the one who sulks, sitting at the back with her arms folded. All the while she would be staring at you like she wants to kill you (she probably did want to kill me!) and sighing, eye rolling and tutting at regular intervals as you put your heart and soul into engaging people with the culture change that you are suggesting for their benefit.

As the workshop progresses, the receptionist becomes more demonstrable, whispering derogatory comments to the people sitting near her and vocalising her scepticism with cynical statements like *"we've heard all this before"* and *"why should we do this when the bosses don't?"* You feel your heart sink and your energy drain as the receptionist's BSF switches on the BSF of those around her because they daren't challenge her and the anti-change sentiment festers around the room. You would end the workshop feeling like you have just been assassinated and held responsible for everything that is bad, even though you're the one who is trying to help others to make positive change.

It would need really strong leadership at "Computers Ltd" to hold the receptionist to account for her negativity and resistance to change. The likelihood is that your dreams of culture change will turn into a nightmare because the leaders' BSF makes them terrified of addressing the receptionist, so your well-thought-out plans for change end up being the latest futile attempt at getting the miserable cow and her followers to be more of a human and less of a BSF-influenced twat.

This is a classic trick of the pesky BSF in an organisation culture as it convinces the people who spend most of their time moaning about how bad it is to work there that nothing will ever change and that everyone else but themselves is to blame. The lack of real cultural change is a perfect demonstration of the BSF in action. Just take a step back and look at it for what it is – people who moan about how bad things are won't change things for themselves and continue to moan about and do the things that they don't like. The attitudes and behaviours that come from a BSF really are completely fucking insane!

There really does need to be a box added to the exit interview form labelled *"Bullshit Factory culture"* that can be ticked as someone's reason for leaving. No organisation wants to be toxic, but it happens as the BSF proliferates the culture. You see the key to a positive culture at work isn't transformational change or projects and initiatives. The key is the authenticity and emotional intelligence it takes to shut down the individual and collective Bullshit Factories that permeate and ruin how it feels to work there.

'Take it from me this life's a reason to make my mind insane.'

– DMA'S

Hijacked by her BSF

The receptionist at "Computers Ltd" is a case study in what happens when your BSF hijacks you and puts you on a journey of inner turmoil and antagonising others. Let's explore the BSF production cycle for our receptionist on the day that I met her.

1. Thoughts and feelings

Kicking off the devil-incarnate receptionist's BSF production cycle, it is very likely that the negative thoughts that she started the day that I met her with would have sounded something like: -

"Today is going to be a bad day.""Nothing is going to go right today."

"Different day, same old shit."

I expect the negative feelings she was experiencing would have been a potent mix of hopelessness, sadness, apprehension, powerlessness and anxiety. With that lethal combination, is it any wonder that I encountered the kind of human being she represented that day? Is it any wonder that she negatively impacts the people she works with?

When combined, the negative thoughts and feelings from your BSF can be intoxicating and you become caught up in this constant fuelling of negativity which becomes your emotions. And your BSF likes to work on repeat and wants you to continuously feed a cycle of doom by chattering away about how you're thinking and feeling so your emotions swallow you up and you end up feeling sad about being sad. You get angry at yourself for being angry. You worry about worrying. You become anxious about feeling anxious and you feel scared about the problems that your thoughts and feelings tell you to expect ahead. Put all those things together and is it any wonder that people slip into becoming like the miserable receptionist I met?

'When you're falling down
And the waves come and crash around
And you sink below all the sounds
From the storm above that's coming down.'

– STEREOPHONICS

2. Self-talk

From those thoughts and feelings, can you even comprehend what the receptionist's self-talk was like? This is where I really empathise with her because she probably felt pecked by her self-talk from morning to night. That negative self-talk is a horrendous thing to live with and gets you stuck in your head. The receptionist was really stuck in her own head with her self-talk beating her up, feeling like a record repetitively spinning things like *"what's the point?"* I dread to think what her self-talk was telling her every time I stood up and walked towards her that fateful morning.

Her BSF would be hijacking her mind, giving her an internal commentary telling her that she had to put up with someone else's shit all day and that there was nothing she could do about it. Worse still, it was probably making her think that it was all her fault and that she had put herself in that situation. Your self-talk really does leave you feeling like you're in a twelve-round fight with peak Mike Tyson as it first tells you that everything is shit and then that *you* are to blame for all that shit. This kind of negative self-talk makes it feel like you're having two different conversations – one with the other person and the other with your internalised thoughts. I would love to get inside her head to hear what her BSF was telling her when I was talking to her. I'd guess that whilst she's saying *"you will need to wait over there"* to me, her self-talk is telling her at the same time *"don't let him get you in trouble"* and *"you've got enough to deal with, don't get involved with his problems"*. That was despite the fact that it was her job to help me solve the problems I was encountering as a visitor.

3. Self-image

As for the receptionist's self-image, that made her fit the mould of being grumpy whilst creating barriers for others. She would have seen herself as someone whose career was going nowhere and that she was stuck in a "dead-end job". The picture in her head on her journey to work (I'm pretty sure that she got dropped off at the office door every morning by the same tornado that sucks up the Wicked Witch of The West!) would have shown her sitting behind a massive reception desk all day being irritable and bothered by everyone and everything. Perversely, even though her self-image is a defeatist one, her BSF will have convinced her that her resistance to other people and avoidance of any type of motivation was inevitable and, therefore, she allowed it to guide her days at work. Kidding herself into thinking of it as some form of protection from her inescapable feeling of being small and insignificant, she continued on this destructive path.

Had she shut down her BSF and asked herself how she wanted to show up and how she wanted her day to go, there is no way she would have chosen what I witnessed. No one sets out to be that much of an arse. It was her BSF running on overtime, putting her down and in turn making her put others down too.

4. Gloom-ridden anticipation

The negative self-image from your BSF turns your anticipation of what will happen next into something that makes you dread every day. It becomes your alarm call that wakes you up in the morning expecting a bad day ahead. It's what prevents you from getting to sleep in the first place because you're worried about what you did today or what will happen tomorrow. Or it suddenly hits you from nowhere in the moment as you react to the situations you find yourself in.

'These are wild, wild,
wild days you live in
Yeah, I know sometimes
we all wanna fit in
These are strange, strange
vein days of living
Yeah, I know sometimes
that ya just don't fit in.'

– RICHARD ASHCROFT

I think by now, you can guess what sort of anticipation of the day ahead our ill-mannered receptionist was experiencing. It's a miracle she even turned up for work, considering what must have been going through her mind from the second she woke up as her BSF made her write the day off before it had even started.

It's safe to say that her BSF was definitely not telling her to look forward to helping visitors feel welcome or support her colleagues when they needed something. Those expectations of our receptionist/antagonist must have been shallow to say the least. Her negative self-fulfilling prophecy would have been a vicious circle of monotonous tasks, only being interrupted by what are to her stupid questions by stupid people. The sum total of what she anticipated to happen next was probably as high as *"well, today is going to be another shit one"*.

'When you look at me, you see what I want you to see
What I want you to see.'

– ARCADE FIRE

5. Attitudes and behaviours

What rolled off the BSF production line for that receptionist also gave me the gift of her story for this book as it had left an indelible mark on me. I have encountered many others operating on a BSF production cycle but that day in sunny Yorkshire stands out above all others. There is not a job description or competency framework in the world that would include the kind of attitudes and behaviours that I faced that morning. At the time of writing this, it is five years since that day in West Yorkshire and I can still vividly remember how her attitudes and behaviours made me feel and the incredulity that ran through my mind in response to the nonsensical way in which she treated me. Her attitudes and behaviours would leave her feeling even more wound up, enflaming the emotions that had triggered them.

I dread to think how she would answer the question *"how was work?"* after another day of her passive-aggressive attitudes and behaviours. No doubt she blamed everyone else. She probably tells her own story about me that morning being the annoying visitor who assumed that she was there to help him. I would be the bad guy who didn't take into consideration that she needed to buy a packet of crisps, describing me asking to enter a meeting room as a personal affront on her.

'Nothing frightens me more than a person unwilling to learn even at their own expense. That's a darkness that really frightens me.'

– G.H. SCOTT FROM "LEAVE THE WORLD BEHIND"

You see the BSF attitudes and behaviours of the receptionist are ones that come from a reactive belief that you are not in control of how you behave and your negative attitudes seep out of you like a leaky bucket. This only pours negativity all over you and anyone else you come into contact with.

The Bullshit Factory is real life for all of us

I was keen to use the receptionist to bring the BSF to life because it is not a theory or an idea that I have dreamt up. It is real. For all of us. I'm sure that whilst reading about the receptionist, you could relate to working with people like her or maybe even see some of yourself in her behaviour. Organisations are full of BSF-powered people and are shaped by the impact they have on colleagues, customers and their entire culture.

I really hope that you are grateful that it's not you in the story experiencing your life through the lens of your BSF. I also wanted to share my receptionist with the world because I genuinely feel for her. I hope her BSF has shown her some mercy since we met and that she has gone back to being who she really wants to be. Whilst I won't ever offer the BSF as an excuse, I truly empathise with people who are in the grip of their BSF and real life for them is an existence of downs and downs. I love helping people to shut down their BSF and feel blessed to have lots of experiences of meeting people who are drowning in their BSF misery but are willing to work hard to shut it down and have a real life that is driven by optimism and a belief that people are good and want to do good by others.

My story of a real BSF in action is by no means a judgement of the receptionist and I hope that sentiment comes across in my writing. People like her are the reason I am writing this book. I want them to know that all is not lost and just because you've had some bad experiences and, like me, possibly lost years to your BSF, it is never too late to shut it down and choose to respond to it in a positive way.

'I'd rather be a hypocrite than the same person forever.'

– ADAM HOROVITZ

What have we done in this chapter

- Seen a real example of how a BSF can turn someone into the "Neggy Nelly" at work
- Experienced how the BSF ruins what should be simple, polite interactions between people
- Witnessed how the BSF can hijack people to make work a negative experience

- Demonstrated how the BSF is one of the biggest barriers to organisational culture
- Explored how the BSF becomes real-life for us

Coaching questions to get you thinking about your BSF...

- How does a Bullshit Factory impact where you work?
- Where does it impact the culture of your organisation?
- What negative attitudes and behaviours have you allowed your BSF to show?
- What is your BSF doing to your thoughts and feelings?
- When is your BSF most "real life" for you?
- How will you make sure that your BSF doesn't ruin your experience of work?

CHAPTER THREE

ME AND MY BULLSHIT FACTORY

'I sometimes think back to
when I was young
To happier times, but now they have gone
I'll try to remember the things
that made me smile
So, here is a story of how it began
How it has gone, and what is the plan
I'll try to remember the things
that made me smile.'

– THE LATHUMS

My BSF on overdrive

"The next train approaching platform 2 doesn't stop here. Please step back from the platform edge," came the announcement at Warrington Bank Quay train station back in 2018.

This is my chance, I thought. *I can walk forward six feet, fall under this train and all my pain ends.* I took a step forward and imagined being relieved of all my worries, perceived inadequacies and how people would feel better off without me in their lives. That anticipation of ending my life felt good and like the inevitable end that I had been building towards.

That is just one vivid memory of me experiencing intense suicidal thoughts. Another one is being in the supermarket holding hands with both of my daughters as we passed the chemist stand, looking down at my kids and telling myself, *"She's six and she's eight. They won't have a clue why I am buying the shed load of over-the-counter pills needed to kill me and put me out of my misery"*. I once spent most of an afternoon sitting at my desk at work surrounded by other people writing on Post-It notes about my plan for taking my own life. I identified a date, place and the combination of alcohol and medication I would need and also wrote out the lies I would tell my wife to excuse me from being at home that night. Around the same time, my commute home from work was spent in complete silence staring blankly at the road ahead as I tried to work myself up to driving off the M60 at Barton Bridge.

'This is how it feels to be lonely
This is how it feels to be small
This is how it feels when your world
means nothing at all.'

– INSPIRAL CARPETS

This is the chapter that is the hardest for me to write. Here, as you might have guessed from that honest start, is where I faced the most fiendish part of my BSF – how it turned my negative thoughts and feelings into a life-threatening battle with my mental health. I will show you how when a BSF is left unchallenged and allowed to control you for a prolonged period, it will take you to the pits of human experience and fill you with despair. Writing this chapter and sharing my story with the world feels like the biggest kicking I can give to my BSF as I declare openly how low it made me and how close I came to ending it all thanks to the BS that poisoned my heart and mind. Most importantly, this is the chapter that will show you the true power of emotional intelligence and, no matter how close you come to the precipice, you can always choose a positive response to come back and shut down your BSF.

These examples I have shared at the start of this chapter weren't isolated incidents. I was consumed by the temptation of killing myself and escaping the negative thoughts and feelings that filled my existence. My suicidal thoughts and genuine determination to end my life were not reserved for bad days, they were omnipresent and were a culmination of my BSF being left on hyper-production.

I would wake up thinking about killing myself. If anything went wrong during the day, even something insignificant, I would console myself with the thought of, *"Oh well, I'm going to end up killing myself anyway so who cares?"*! And then my days would end with my BSF keeping me up all night telling me that I was useless and that I just needed to hurry up and end my life. During the worst of these times, I went to work in the morning having not slept for a single minute. I would spend the following day feeling in a complete daze like a zombie with a speech bubble above his head that read, *"Everyone will be better off without you. No-one will miss you. You need to kill yourself"*.

And if that wasn't enough, the even madder thing for me looking back is that I still functioned and still performed at work. I was the master at hiding my misery and desperation. Luckily, I wear glasses so I had them to hide the bags under my eyes.

To everyone around me, I was still me – engaging with people, having a laugh, contributing to meetings and standing up in front of rooms full of people facilitating an event or a workshop. I remember one day that I launched a new Inspiring Performance programme to over 50 people, including the CEO, having had zero hours of sleep the night before. It was one of my lowest points. Still, I simply dusted myself off, put my gear on and got on with it. Then I drove home convinced that tomorrow I would finally kill myself.

Sure, during this dark time, I would sometimes have the odd grumpy mood swing and people would ask me if I was OK or call me out for being a bit short with them. I would give it the old *"Yeah, I'm fine, thanks"* or pass it off with some lame excuse about being a man or that I was pissed off about something trivial. All the while, inside I was screaming at them *"I WANT TO FUCKING KILL MYSELF. YOU WOULD BE IN A BAD MOOD TOO IF YOU WERE INSIDE MY HEAD"*.

I often wonder how many other people are practising being the "great pretender" to hide what their BSF is doing to them? Perhaps some of them work with you? Perhaps it is you? The BSF is a master of deception, making people want to appear like everything is "fine" when inside they are fighting the biggest battle of their lives.

'I've never really ever met a normal person.'

– ARCADE FIRE

All the time that I was in the throes of doom, I just thought that it was normal! At least, it was normal for me anyway. My BSF made me believe that this was it and that the rest of my life was going to be accompanied with suicidal thoughts. And it made me accept it, with a whimsical *"Oh well, that's life, isn't it?"* attitude as I awaited the day when I would finally pluck up the courage to go through with my plans to kill myself. There was no way that I was going to speak to someone or tell them how I was thinking or feeling because my BSF put up a big fuck off barrier preventing me from doing that. It was like a humongous gate with *"no-one needs to hear about your problems"* and *"you need to MAN UP"* painted on it blocking my path and stopping me from getting help.

Spending time with my wife and kids or going out with family and friends would be like out-of-body experiences for me as I put on a brave face and didn't show any sign of weakness, when internally I felt like I was somewhere else. I would spend what was supposed to be a good time for me, repeatedly telling myself that no-one wants me here and that I just need to get through it and then I can focus on my suicide and be free from all the pain. It was like I was living a double life as other people saw me as the same old Tim whereas I saw myself as someone who detested everything about the same old Tim.

This is what your BSF can do to you. The people I worked with and my family and friends weren't telling me that I was bad to be around. They still wanted to spend time with me and had no idea what was going on inside me, but my BSF was on a propaganda overdrive. It made me think that I was worthless and that it was normal to think that way. It gave me complete misery to carry around and told me to be embarrassed about how I felt so it could stop me from telling anyone else. It made me think that the people who love me didn't want me around and that I had somehow let them down. Those years when I was completely hijacked by my BSF were the worst years of my life and I wouldn't wish them on anyone else.

'Understand it's part of me
where all this fades away
Tomorrow morning's back again, I'm
singing through the pain.'

– DMA'S

My BSF ruined my mental health

What I have shared with you here isn't me trying to dumb down my serious issues or use the BSF as an excuse for poor mental health. I use the concept of my BSF to win my ongoing battle with my mental health challenges because it helps me to understand that what it made me think and feel and how it made me behave were total BS. I don't want to feel down. I don't want to think that I am worthless. I don't want to believe that my wife and kids are better off without me. And I definitely don't want to kill myself. Yet my BSF made all of those things normal for me. That's the power this invisible enemy has over you.

I love being around people. I believe in people. I love having a laugh. I really give a shit about doing a good job. I am naturally optimistic and believe that tomorrow will be even better than today. I have a good life with lots of friends and family around me. I am healthy. I love my job. I love my daughters with an amount of love that is impossible to describe. I am married to my best mate who makes me laugh every day. I go to gigs and football matches all the time and play golf (badly) with my best mate in the summer. I have a fantastic collection of clothes, books and records (what else is there to spend your money on?). I have brilliant parents who are great company and who give me good advice. Despite all of those things that make me a very lucky human being, I went through hell with my mental health thanks to my BSF.

'Everybody's asking me if I'm alright
But I don't have the guts to say it.'

– SAM FENDER

Spoiler alert – you are reading this book which means that I got help and am now winning my battle with my negative mental health.

When I did finally get help, I was diagnosed by a GP. It's an equation of anxiety + stress = severe depression. When I got my initial diagnosis, my BSF really enjoyed itself as the GP pulled out a Yellow Pages of drugs and offered me anti-depressants, despite me telling her that was the last thing I wanted. Then I was offered the chance to be referred for Anger Management Classes. I wasn't angry, I was depressed! Is it any wonder that so many people are consumed by their Bullshit Factories? When I first sought out help and was diagnosed with severe depression, it gave my BSF "proof" that I was a fuck up and even my doctor couldn't help me!

'Am I strong enough?
Oh, tell me, am I strong enough?
Oh, gotta tell me, am I strong enough?'

– RAY LAMONTAGNE

My emotional intelligence saved my life

I don't share my mental health experiences to shock you. For me, my life was a BSF-fuelled misery for years. There were days when I literally couldn't get out of bed due to being completely consumed with depression. 2018 was off the charts for me in terms of my depression and I look back now and can't believe I survived to share my story. 2018 was also the year that things changed for me and I took control and shut down my BSF.

In the summer of that year, I was given the opportunity to speak at the CIPD Coaching Conference in London – my biggest speaking gig to date at that time. For a coach and someone working in Learning and Development, it was a massive moment – the pinnacle for anyone who believes in coaching and wants to be known as a trusted speaker. I was contacted by the events company who were running the event on behalf of CIPD and asked to be one of their keynote speakers. I can remember being so happy when I went home to tell my wife about it and it felt like there was finally a ray of sunshine breaking through the black clouds of my depression.

The weeks leading up to the Conference gave me something to focus on and empowered me to ignore my BSF still nagging away at me with suicidal prompts. I felt like I was getting treated as a VIP on calls with the organisers. They wanted me to be the opening speaker and they also asked me to join an Expert Panel for a slot later on in the day. They sent me the details of the 5-Star hotel in Chelsea that I was staying in and I allowed myself to believe that things might just be OK after all.

In the run-up to the conference, I had a little wobble and doubted myself and questioned whether my honest, no-BS approach needed to be replaced with a more corporate, sanitised version that my BSF was telling me the audience wanted. Would they just reject me as the token Northerner who didn't know what he was talking about? I sought out my trusted mate Danny Seals (love you Danny) who listened to me and gave me some precious pointers on my talk. I told Danny what I was thinking about taking a different approach to my talk and he took a big intake of breath, looked at me and told me *"Take your own advice, Tim"* with a smile on his face, knowing exactly what I would say if the tables were turned. That gave me the kick up the arse I needed and that simple reply has remained immensely impactful for me ever since.

'And he's refreshing the world in mind,
body and spirit
Mind, body and spirit,
you'd better hear it not fear it.
Ah, that's the spirit.'

– FONTAINES D.C.

The day of the conference arrived and I felt amazing, unbelievably confident. It was like I couldn't believe that I could feel so good about myself and be so excited to do something that felt so big. I had lots of good luck messages from my wife and friends and I felt like I was walking on air as I entered the Conference Suite. As the room started to fill up with hundreds of people who were attending, I didn't feel nervous and just had this weird sense that I was going to smash my talk and really enjoy myself. I had practised and worked really hard to get to this point and was ready for the spotlight to be on me.

And smash it I did! I mean, I absolutely fucking smashed it. It was one of those moments in your life when you feel invincible and that you deserve to be up there on stage shining amongst your peers. I stuck to my guns and my principles and did the talk in my own style and I had the room in the palm of my hands for the 30 minutes of my talk. I even used my infamous line that has gone down in CIPD folklore as I told the crowd that *"you can stick your Annual Appraisal right up your arse"*, which I think secured the standing ovation that I got from the whole room. I looked at Jo, who looked at me with a face beaming with pride and gave me a double thumbs up.

This was like a positive out-of-body feeling for me. After months of my BSF getting so close to beating me into fatal submission, I had bounced back and taken a gigantic step towards what I wanted to do moving forward. The rest of the conference was a glorious experience for me as people congratulated me on my talk and wanted to ask me lots of questions. Some of the people I met that day are now clients of mine who I have worked with for many years. The speaker who followed me said, *"I can't believe I had to follow you, Tim. You are an impossible act to follow."* The absolute icing on the cake was when the conference host, Stuart, thanked me for making the day and told me, *"I'm pretty sure that no-one has ever said the word 'arse' on stage at a CIPD Conference before, Tim."* As my confidence was sky-rocketing by that stage, I replied with, *"They have now, Stuart."* He replied with a big belly-laugh and shook my hand before telling me that I had to be a guest on his coaching podcast.

The conference ended and I made my way back to Euston and such was my confidence that I didn't even feel scared of using the tube (I'm a Northerner remember!). I checked my LinkedIn and it felt like I had broken the internet as I had so many notifications and new connection requests in response to my talk. I grabbed a couple of my favourite beers for the train home and sat there surrounded by strangers listening to my tunes and reading my book as I floated all the way home. I made sure to allow a moment to take it all in and told myself, *"Whatever happens now, no-one can ever take today away from me. I DID IT"*.

'We'll fall down, we'll fall down
Don't know how, don't look down
This dream of where's to
Keep on keepin' on.'

– STEREOPHONICS

Me telling you about my victory at the CIPD Coaching Conference is not an attempt at self-promotion or to gloss over my mental health issues revealed earlier in the chapter. Even now, my BSF would rather me write that in a self-deprecating way and, as I revisit that time, I look back with incredulity that it was actually me who brought the house down and delivered a talk by taking a risk to say it as it is only to have hundreds of people agreeing with me. It is an example of the strength that we can find when we shut down our BSF. Back then, I didn't know that was what I was doing because my BSF had blinded me. My BSF was invisible to me then as I just thought I was another "normal person" living a miserable internal existence. This particular episode with my BSF is also really important because it became the catalyst for change and made me take on the fight to shut down my BSF.

I returned to work the day after the conference and, for once, I was really looking forward to going into the place that was a potent trigger for the depressive antics of my BSF. I walked into the office still buzzing from my talk and, as I saw people, it felt like they knew how good I had been and how amazing I felt and I couldn't stop smiling.

I was first in that day and sat at my desk still going through all the activity on my LinkedIn as more and more notifications flooded in sharing positive comments and messages about me being the star of the show at the conference. My colleagues started to arrive and I expected a hero's return and waited for them to ask me about my talk and all the coverage on social media. After all, I had appeared at a landmark CIPD Conference representing the organisation and the People Team that I was part of. And then it started…

Nothing. Not a mention. Not even a lazy *"How was London?"* from any of them. An hour or so passed and all of the team were now in, including my boss, and there was not a murmur from any of them. They knew that I was doing the talk, and they must have seen it on LinkedIn, and yet not a single one of them bothered to ask me or pass any positive comments to me. Instead, they all got excited to hear the latest gossip from one team member about their disaster of a BS Tinder date the night before. At which point, I slipped away to grab a brew and go and waste ten minutes chatting to a lad about football to compose myself as I felt the darkness starting to gather again.

I went back to my desk, put my headphones in and got on with some work to take my mind off the disappointment that I felt at being ghosted by my colleagues. I then got a tap on the shoulder from my boss who smiled at me as I took out my headphones. I got a brief tinge of excitement as I thought the ignorance of the team was all a ruse and they were about to surprise me with a gesture of support and recognition. It was another classic example of how your BSF makes you feel like a total pillock as I could not have been further from the truth. Instead, I was told, *"I need to catch up with you about the GDPR training. Can we do it now as you don't look busy and I've got a meeting in fifteen minutes?"*

I mustered up a *"yes"* as my heart sank and my BSF appeared again on my internal horizon, waving at me, saying *"As if you're that good. No-one cares about your talk. Go on, into the boss's office to be put in your place, you miserable dickhead."* I sloped off behind my manager with my whole body and mind giving out a deflated internal sigh and I started to feel the heaviness of my depression kicking back in.

'Just another lost soul,
trying to feel something
In the age of anxiety.'

– ARCADE FIRE

I walked into my boss's office where I faced a monologue: another attempt at patronising me to assert her authority. I half-listened as she told me about some idiot somewhere in the organisation making a passing comment to her about GDPR training which she now had to pass on to me and demand an update. God forbid she actually sticks up for her team and remembers that the training was actually going really well. I just sat there staring at the floor, nodding and occasionally saying *"yes"*. The best I could do was tell her that I would sort it out as I just wanted to be out of there, to retreat to the perceived solace of thinking about killing myself.

The next few hours were a blur of me sinking into my chair, just clicking through different things on my laptop without actually doing anything. It was like when they speed up the passing by of other people in a film scene whilst the main character stays perfectly still, time passing them by as they lose themselves in their own thoughts and feelings. I cannot explain coherently enough how horrendous it was for a human being to be engrossed by the thoughts and feelings that swamped me in those few hours and it was amplified by having gone from the maximum high of the day before to now returning into a deep, dark hole of misery. I got another e-mail from LinkedIn with more positive reaction to my talk and, instead of logging in and enjoying the adulation, I went straight into the settings and hovered my finger over "delete account". My BSF tightened its grip, telling me that I was a waste of space who didn't deserve any more positive experiences; yesterday was just a freak of nature, a fluke never to be repeated.

You see, this was *the day* that I spent most of an afternoon sitting at my desk in work surrounded by other people as I wrote on Post-It notes my plan for taking my own life. It was the day I mentioned earlier on. Can you imagine how bad someone must feel to go from floating on air to planning their suicide using Post-Its in less than 24 hours?

"Making positive choices is where it all starts for shutting down your BSF — It Always Starts With You"

'Couldn't find a way out of my worried mind.'

– PAOLO NUTINI

My BSF turning point

As absurd as it might sound, that was the turning point for me. As I turned to another Post-It, for some reason, I lifted my head up and looked out of the window. I don't know what made me do it. Maybe it was the tune I was listening to (thank you Paolo Nutini) or maybe it was something within me that made me realise I had to fight my way out of the hole. Or maybe it was a flicker of something from the day before. Whatever it was, it kicked me and made me respond to my thoughts and feelings and reach for the life ring.

I stared out of that window and started to feel lucky to be where I was. For all its pretence and the lying bastards, the office had a beautiful view of the Manchester skyline. In that very moment, the scene on the horizon was one that only Manchester can give you. I saw the rain clouds start to drift away and visible rays of sunshine broke through to light up the skyscrapers and the Pennines in the background. This wasn't an epiphany. The music and the Mancunian vista certainly helped but, in that moment, something inside of me snapped and I was done with feeling like shit and being in a perpetual sense of helplessness. Maybe the production cycle of my BSF stalled for a brief moment. Maybe Danny's words of *"Take your own advice, Tim"* slipped through the manufacturing process and I saw my chance. It was the chance to choose what products came from within me and I was determined to choose a positive response to my thoughts and feelings, changing my attitudes and behaviours as a result.

I stood up and threw the entire pad of Post-Its in the bin, picked up my laptop and walked away from my desk. I went to the late-afternoon quiet of the "social zone" (more BS for what used to be called the canteen) and sat there and wrote a different plan. A plan for how to turn my life around and break out of my prison of depression. I sat and wrote a letter to my wife telling her how I was feeling and being open about my suicidal thoughts. I admitted my depression ("admitted" because as usual my wife was right and had told me months earlier that she thought I was depressed. At the time, thanks to my BSF, I angrily contested and told her that I just wasn't feeling well and was having a bad day). I told her that I knew that I needed help. I emailed the letter to my wife and told her that I was ready to talk. I then walked out of work, oblivious to whether it was actually time to leave or not, and that night, my wife and I talked and my turnaround truly started.

'Took for granted all the things I forgot I know.'

– STEREOPHONICS

The next day, I told my boss a little white lie so I could work from home. It was the first time in a long time that I remembered having a choice and not having to play to her tune as she clearly didn't give a toss about me anyway. I made an appointment with my GP (back in the days when you could ring up and do that in the morning!) and, even though that didn't go to plan in terms of getting meaningful help, hearing her say the words *"You're suffering from severe depression, Mr Roberts"* meant so much to me and gave me something to fight, something that enabled me to make sense of the BS that was going round and round in my head, ruining my days and nights.

I took on that fight and, over the coming weeks, I shared my depression with my family who all understood and supported me. I also talked to my mates about it and we went from blokes in a pub talking about football and putting the world to rights to blokes in a pub talking about my depression and how bad it had gotten for me. Every single one of them was supportive and remain that way to this day. I remember shitting myself about telling my best mate as I wanted to make sure I told him before anyone else, and he really listened to me. No judgments, no piss-taking. He just listened and told me he understood and was there for me.

'Say something, say something, anything.'

– JAMES

Those conversations spurred me on and I chose to take on the fight with the depression that my BSF gave me. One of my mates told me *"You've got to keep fighting, Tim. Keep swimming, mate"*, in reference to swimming out of the deep, treacherous waters of depression, and I continue to use that as a motto today. I accept that I will have depression for the rest of my life and now welcome the fight and use it to motivate me.

A surprising bonus is that sharing my mental health battles made my BSF retreat. It doesn't like being talked about and shies away from conflict if it thinks you can respond to it with motivation and a positive outlook. It will hate the fact that you're reading about it now in a book that exposes its deviance to the world. Even just reading this sentence will start to dampen down your BSF. Like all bullies, it has no backup when it is faced with an army of people who care for you and want you to kick its head in. I took strength from talking to my family and friends. I even did some public speaking at events, sharing my experiences with depression and taking my story out to the world to show my BSF that whilst it had won many battles, it was not going to win the war with me.

The office Post-Its became a positive weapon for me as I now planned my escape from the awful place where I worked, which had provided so much fuel for my BFS. I moved swiftly towards a world where I was in control, creating opportunities for me to have the autonomy and enjoyment that my BSF hates me to have. I decided that I was going to be the controller and not the controlled, removing the self-deception that my BSF is a master of so I could make positive choices to shut it down.

'I wanna get happy before I get old.'

– PAOLO NUTINI

Whilst talking about my knackered mental health gave me momentum and a tangible action towards starting to shut down my BSF, it was choosing to talk about it that was the real trigger for my turnaround. The positive power I took from my conversations was all down to me first choosing a positive response to my thoughts and feelings. For years, I did pretty much everything that my thoughts and feelings told me to do. The severe depression and desire for suicide was a culmination of years of my BSF pushing me harder and harder so it beat me down over a long time. This made my BSF grow stronger and that turned me into a pushover who had weak defences against the persistent beatings from my BSF.

Making positive choices is where it all starts for shutting down your BSF – It Always Starts With You.

This is where my emotional intelligence saved my life. It was my emotional intelligence that kicked in that day when I binned the suicidal Post-Its; it made me see the light. It reminded me that I have the power to choose. I always had it. I just needed a nudge to remember it was there in my armoury and I had to *"take my own advice"*. Your emotional intelligence is how you recognise, understand and choose a positive response to your thoughts and feelings. It is how you choose your attitudes and behaviours to be your best version of you. My BSF had tricked me into forgetting about this greatest power and, even though I had spent years developing mine and helping others to develop theirs, my BSF stopped me from applying it.

I used my new-found motivation to make positive choices and put my emotional intelligence into action through the different capabilities that it gives to us humans: -

- **Self-awareness** – I worked really hard on understanding who I am and what I stand for so I could align my attitudes and behaviours to that. I chose to recognise and understand my emotions and the thoughts and feelings that come from them. This helped me to spot when the anxiety or stress was kicking in and respond to it before it tipped into my depression.

- **Self-management** – I reminded myself that I can control my emotions, both proactively and in the moment. Whilst my BSF would still prompt emotional reactions that sent me into depression, I could now choose to respond differently and not allow my emotions to switch on my negative autopilot. I learnt to self-coach so my self-talk was regularly met with a positive response and I challenged myself to talk to myself in a way that didn't destroy my confidence and instead spurred me on to do what I really wanted to do.

- **Social awareness** – I paid more attention to the impact I was having on others and proactively chose what I wanted that to be. I chose to tune in to others and pay attention to what was going on for them. Rather than jumping to the tune of the people who didn't care about me, I learnt to choose a positive response to allow their attitudes and behaviours to reflect on them and not negatively influence me.

- **Relationship Management** – I stopped wasting time and energy on the relationships that brought me no joy and were only serving the other person. I consciously chose to put my ambition into action and got out there meeting new people and building networks that inspired me and were built on trust. I remembered that I exist to help me and my family and not serve the purpose of the dickheads. I put my true, authentic self into my relationships, which completely turned things around for me, and I was met with reciprocal positive attitudes and behaviours from others.

I may have glossed over the real work that I did a little there and the above is only a high-level summary of the hard graft that I put into developing and applying my emotional intelligence. That journey from the edge of the proverbial cliff to getting back to being myself was a very tough one and not without its bumps along the way. We will do a deep dive into how to shut down your BSF in a later chapter.

Ultimately, it is the work you put into your emotional intelligence that will enable you to win your fight with your own BSF.

'Nothing is perfect
No-one is perfect
Let me say it again;
no-one's perfect.'

– ARCADE FIRE

My BSF tormented me for years

The road to severe depression was long and winding. I didn't just end up there, I spent years with my BSF in charge, which culminated in it hammering my mental health. I guess the depression came from the complete exhaustion of allowing my BSF to determine what happened to me and how I felt about my experiences. For many years, the production cycle of my BSF was this:

Production Line	1. My **thoughts and feelings** were a hotbed of negativity. 2. My **self-talk** told me that I shouldn't develop myself. It told me not to try to progress and that I should wait for someone else to decide if I was ready to be promoted or not. A thought that repeated itself was "what's the point?" At work, it made me hell-bent on controlling everything and everyone around me, telling me that no-one else could be trusted to do their job. 3. My **self-image** was one of being stuck in dead-end jobs (I wasn't!) and that I had let myself and my family down by not doing better for myself. I saw myself as the cause of all of my perceived problems and as someone who couldn't get anything right. It made me feel like I was carrying around a massive weight of sadness and frustration. It made me see myself as someone who was on a path to disappointment with my career and life. 4. My **gloom-ridden anticipation** was something that I wouldn't wish on anyone. I just expected every day to be full of problems and that everyone who I worked with would either dislike me, disagree with me or show me up in some way. I was convinced that what happened today was going to happen tomorrow and that I was consigned to a world of misery. I began each day filled with dread, anticipating a bad day ahead. Even when something positive like the CIPD Conference happened, I would soon revert to negativity. I was truly living the negative self-fulfilling prophecy.

Products	5. My **attitudes and behaviours** were sometimes off the scale. I could be the office keyboard warrior and moody manager all rolled into one. I would lie awake at night looking back at my day and asking myself *"Why did I say that?"* and then go back to work the day after and do it all over again. I was a cracking micromanager and couldn't wait for the chance to catch people out for not doing something and then try to chastise or patronise them in front of other people. I prepared for meetings by gathering evidence to prove people wrong and would do everything I could to show people that I was right. Listening was not an option for me and 1-2-1's with me would be a "1". I did all the talking telling people what I thought and what they should do. I would force myself to work late and some weekends to try and cover up my ineptitude just to try and show that I was busy and would take responsibility. There were so many occasions when how I behaved at work was so far away from how I behaved out of work. It was like I had my very own Jekyll and Hyde going on.

'And more dead than alive
And my feelings
They've always been betrayed
And I was born a little damaged man.'

– THE VERVE

Looking at that BSF Production Cycle, it's no wonder that I sleep-walked into depression. I spent around two years of my career being the assassin for a boss who would bark orders at me to go and kick my team for anything that went wrong. I would be summoned into her office, take the latest bollocking and then go out and take that out on my team. I wouldn't listen to their responses and would simply leave a trail of destruction behind me. I did this while knowing, deep down, that what I was doing was wrong, but I still did it anyway. I ignored my bad feelings and chose to ignore the impact I was having on my own team as long as I could appease my boss. I was oblivious to how weak this made me look as a leader and how I actually created zero accountability with my team because they knew that I would always tell them what to do and how to do it.

I also spent a large chunk of my time laughing at a boss's inappropriate jokes, which bordered on sexist and racist half the time. My BSF had me in such a vice-like grip that I ignored my conscience and instead approved of this abhorrent behaviour by not calling it out. I did this because my BSF convinced me that I was safer condoning my despicable boss to protect me from putting my head above the parapet and following the attitudes and behaviours of those other leaders around me who I would never choose to be like.

'The most powerful voice you will ever hear is the one inside your head.'

– ROB JOHNSON

You can't click your fingers to shut down your BSF

I got to the point in 2018 where I was riddled with severe depression and the act of choosing to save my own life came from years of starting to shut down my BSF. It is a gradual process and one that needs acceptance. You must first accept your BSF and remind yourself that you are human. One of the first things I did was to make peace with the fact that, like all other humans, I am not perfect. I will have bad days and I will have times when my thoughts and feelings are not ones that I would choose for myself. I embrace my BSF and, even though that will not stop it from firing up, it removes the fear of it. Instead of feeling powerless, like I did for many years, I know that I can shut it down by choosing a positive response to it.

I chose to shut down my BSF because it was ruining my life. It was making me think that my leadership roles, which I'd worked hard to get to, were a burden and that I should give up. It told me to wait until someone else said I was ready to be promoted or someone else decided what role would be for me. They would guide how I should approach my career.

It always starts with you so you have to choose to shut down your BSF if you want to be the best version of you that you can be. Shutting down your BSF is one of the most practical and powerful things that your emotional intelligence enables you to do. My life can very much be seen through the "before and after" lens for when my BSF was in charge and when I started to shut it down. Here are some of the different positive responses that I choose to use to shut it down:

My BSF in control	Shutting it Down
➡ Natural thoughts and feelings telling me that every day was going to be a bad day.	➡ Telling myself that today is a good day and the only thing I need to do is be myself.
➡ Following the bad examples of others to protect myself from the risk of doing things differently.	➡ Spending time to get absolute clarity on who I am and what I stand for and what I will tolerate and what I won't.
➡ Beating myself up for mistakes and not being perfect. Ruminating over things I wish I had done better.	➡ Only judging my success on whether my attitudes and behaviours live up to what I stand for.
➡ Lack of confidence in myself as a leader.	➡ Self-coach and ask myself *"How do I want to come across today?"*
➡ Convinced that all meetings are going to be negative, that I won't be able to speak up and be left regretting what happened.	➡ Self-coach and ask myself *"What do I want to get from this meeting?"* and *"How do I want to feel after this meeting?"*
➡ Go into conversations telling myself that I know what other people are going to say and not listening to them.	➡ Tell myself that I never know what people are going to say until they say it!

The biggest change for me when shutting down my BSF was going back to being me. That is what my BSF took away from me. Everything changed when I went back to being me, making positive choices based on who I really am and what's right for me (not the Tim that's trying to fit in). The impact on my confidence levels was exponential and it motivated me to work in a way where the most important thing was choosing my attitudes and how I wanted to behave. The only measure I put on anything now is whether I can walk away from any situation happy that how I came across aligned to who I am and whether I lived up to what I stand for.

'Times were tough, we made it through
We tasted the rough,
so let's savour the smooth
All the time I was hurting you
Got to believe that I was hurting, too.'

– RAY LAMONTAGNE

Even when you're shutting it down, it can kick you in the guts

Even though I have completed my turnaround and shut down my BSF, it won't stop it from playing dirty tricks on me and it still comes back to haunt me sometimes. I'm not telling you this to frighten you or suggest that working on shutting it down is a waste of time. It is a really important reminder that you have to be consistent; you can't ever allow yourself to be complacent and think "That's it. I've sussed it and my BSF is shut down forever". Your heart and mind are just not that kind to you. The more I work on shutting down my BSF, the more resilient I become and the more quickly I am able to step out of its grasp and choose a positive response.

Post my 2018 nightmare, I still have some disaster episodes with my BSF but, by choosing to positively respond, I come back even stronger and ready to commit to the long-term, consistent habits that I need to practise to keep it at bay, along with the more responsive challenges too. I need to spring into action when it fires up on any particular day that it decides to be the slippery, conniving sod that it is.

When your BSF pulls you away from being yourself

I've admitted already that my BSF encouraged me to laugh at the offensive jokes my boss made when that wasn't me at all. Mid-way through 2019, my BSF came very close to forcing me to do something that is so not me, and it took my wife to pull me out of it.

Picture the scene. It was mid-2019 and I was flying. I had broken free from the hell I used to work in and was instead living the dream by working for myself. I was building my reputation and my business and working with lots of different organisations and coaching clients. Here I was, still in the same world that my BSF ruined for me, full of confidence and bordering on feeling invincible as I delivered more and more coaching and leadership development.

I got a call from a friend of mine who told me about a new TedTalk event launching close to me and encouraged me to apply to be a speaker. This wasn't even on my horizon and I had never considered applying to do a TedTalk as it just wasn't something that I thought would help me to keep doing what I am doing. My BSF told me to jump at the opportunity as this is what entrepreneurs that are better than you would do – this is how you grow your business. But my BSF told me to fit a mould of what a successful entrepreneur does when, in my heart, I knew all along that it just wasn't me. However, my BSF won by telling me to ignore my instincts and convinced me that the opportunity to tell people that I was doing a TedTalk was exactly what I wanted.

I applied and got selected to be a speaker at the launch event for the new TedTalk franchise and, even though one of the things that was stressed to us at the first speaker meeting and in the contract I signed was that we mustn't tell anyone about the event until it was launched on the TedTalk social channels, I set about telling everyone I could that I was doing a TedTalk. I told my mates about it even though some of them have never heard of TedTalks and don't care about the work I do because they care about me and not what I do!

Short of plastering it all over LinkedIn and taking out an ad in the local paper, anyone I met was told with great misplaced pride coming from my BSF how I was going to be a TedTalk speaker and that they must come to the event when it goes live. I couldn't wait until I could add "TedTalk Speaker" to my LinkedIn profile and share the video of my talk on YouTube.

As the process started and the time commitment I would have to make became clear, I started to get very anxious and worry about the guidelines being given to us. I knew that TedTalks came with a lot of guidance to adhere to. Of course, they do. It's part of what makes them so successful and I completely respect them. TedTalks had to protect its global brand, which meant very tight guidelines on how you could deliver your talk. I get it: TedTalks are massive and they give a platform to millions of people across the world. I love TedTalks and how much they help people. But I don't work well with strict guidelines (you know me, I like to Break the Mould)! Having to fit into someone else's parameters was like it was sent from heaven to my BSF when I worked in organisations. I need autonomy and have to be able to be myself and feel trusted to do a good job because my need for personal integrity is off the fucking scale.

I also cannot ever feel like I let someone down or that I don't put 100% into what I do as I am a grafter and love working hard to help others and have a good time whilst doing it. So, as I attended more speaker meetings and got introduced to the many additional guidelines within which I would have to do my talk, my levels of stress intensified. I had a knot in my stomach and felt like a bus was parked on my chest every time I started to write my talk. Two of the guidelines were:

- No swearing
- No moving about the stage – you must stay on the red X

My no BS approach doesn't lend itself to bland, corporate language and seeing as using the word *"arse"* at the CIPD Conference launched me into a positive world then I couldn't see how I could dampen down my passionate approach without the odd use of real language. I don't want to say things like *"fuck"*, *"shit"* and *"bollocks"* for a laugh or a gimmick – that's how I talk and it is how people relate to me amongst a world of coaches and speakers who sound like they have swallowed the same business dictionary.

I also don't like standing still on stage. It flattens my energy and I am a firm believer that demonstrative body language and the occasional walk across the stage keeps your audience engaged and shows confidence. Anyone can stand behind a lectern or on a red X and I don't want to be like everyone else (*"that's why I'm a Mod, see?"* – if you know then you know). I can't even stand still when practising my talks in front of my cat, Tigger, because my enthusiasm comes from my motion on stage.

It was starting to feel very off. I knew this wasn't for me, but my BSF told me that I had to go through with it now and that I had to change myself and my whole approach because it was a massive opportunity. It put me under huge pressure to commit the time, turning down work to attend all meetings and practice runs just to be able to say that I had done a TedTalk.

On top of the suffocating guidelines, I felt that the people who were organising the TedTalk event and all of the other speakers were just not my kind of people. Nice people and very professional but just not my kind of gang. I felt very out of place at the meetings and could not relate to them at all. They were all motivated by very different things to me and I felt completely alienated in some of the conversations that took place. How they talked about other people made me squirm and I just couldn't get on board with the self-aggrandising going on around the room as they competed for attention and to tell each other how successful they were. I remember one speaker (who admitted that her TedTalk was going to be her first ever go at public speaking!!) giving me some feedback on my first practice that was genuinely about as much use to me as a chocolate teapot.

'And heaven knows I'm miserable now.'

– THE SMITHS

The whole experience was ruining my days. Even when I was working with brilliant clients, doing what I love, all the while I had a nagging feeling in the back of my mind about the pending TedTalk. It reached a crescendo the day before I was going on holiday with my wife and kids. I spent the day re-working my talk because I had to submit my updated notes and slides before going away.

This was the first holiday that we had booked since I started working for myself and was really important family time. However, the day before going on holiday, I was a grumpy, cantankerous twat to my wife and kids, refusing to help with the packing or excitement of going to Cornwall and instead bashing away on my laptop whilst my BSF convinced me that my TedTalk was more important than my family.

As the day wore on and my wife tried for the umpteenth time to ask me about the holiday, I snapped at her and screamed *"Do you not know how important this is to me? I need to concentrate"*. My wife snapped back at me and rightly called out the BSF-sized elephant in the room by holding me to account with an assertive *"If it's that important to you then why is it making you speak to me and the kids like this?"*. She walked out of the room and, in that moment, my BSF made me believe that she was wrong and I was right and I gave the classic, immature response of sticking the V's up at the door that she had just slammed shut on me.

That heated exchange with my wife left an impression on me and I just sat there staring at my laptop and felt really low. My emotional intelligence kicked in. I asked myself *"Why am I doing this?"* It was the first time I had questioned my own hype that was coming from my BSF and I started to realise that what I was trying to do just wasn't me. I don't want to feel like this and I don't want my time to be consumed with something that wouldn't show me in the best light. I needed my wife to hold the mirror up to me to question what I was doing and my choices. I started to feel the weight of the whole thing starting to lift as I asked myself if I really needed to do it, which opened up the possibility of making the right choice for me. I wouldn't be letting anyone down by pulling out as they had reserve speakers who would step in. In fact, they would be delighted and were much more likely to be the kind of people they wanted anyway. And more importantly, by doing it, I would be letting my wife and kids down with my BSF-driven behaviours.

I began to recognise that I was trying to do something that massively conflicted with what I believe. On top of that, I was working so hard on it that it was taking my attention away from what was actually important. I realised that I would feel prouder of myself for choosing to not put myself through more anxiety and stress just to be able to tell people that I had done a TedTalk. I realised that this was never part of my plan and that it wasn't the kind of personal branding that I wanted for myself. TedTalks is a fantastic brand and I still avidly watch many of their talks. Being one of their speakers is just not for me and that's OK.

The anticipation of getting myself out of a commitment that I never really wanted to make in the first place filled me with more excitement than I had felt at any stage over the last few months since I signed up to do the TedTalk.

I closed down my talk notes and slides and opened up an e-mail to the organisers and wrote a very polite e-mail in my own words notifying them of my decision and wished them all the best for the event. I signed off with a line that firmly shut down my BSF as I explained that *"The bottom line is that I don't want to do a TedTalk; I want to do a TimTalk".* I didn't need to wait too long to know I had done the right thing as I never even got a reply from the organisers to acknowledge my decision – definitely not my kind of people!

Your BSF can get you very close to doing the things that you don't actually want to do and push you to go against what you stand for. The best thing about that whole experience was walking into the room where my wife and kids were to tell her that she was right and that I had pulled out. Telling the people who are most important to me that I had stopped myself from going through a stressful experience so I could be who I really am meant the world to me. It gave me a far bigger buzz than standing on a red X in some leisure centre talking to an audience mostly made up of the friends and family members of the people who I never wanted to see again! I never will be able to add "TedTalk Speaker" to my LinkedIn profile and that is alright with me.

'I wanna get happy before I get old.'

– PAOLO NUTINI

Know your triggers

Like for the whole world, 2020 was a shitter of a year for me. The Coronavirus induced lockdowns gave me a world of negative emotions that included a playlist of feeling: -

- Sad
- Unwanted
- Useless
- Without purpose
- Pointless
- Lazy
- Bored
- Uncertain
- Ignored

My BSF was busier than ever that year, and the depression kicked back in with my morning walks (remember when we were only allowed outside for an hour a day?!) often following a sleepless night. My BSF blinkered my understanding of what was really triggering the cocktail of negative emotions and made me blame everything on Covid and the restrictions it placed on us. I was Chief Covid Complainer and would spend all day working remotely with groups of people and still feel incredibly lonely. My evening routine was one of rushing to watch the news and then bitching and moaning about it all and telling my wife how unfair it was on me because I worked for myself and my work was all about being with people. I completely ignored how my wife and kids felt about it and made my frustration with being trapped at home negatively impact them. I would go to bed every night full of negativity and then wake up the next day expecting another day of apathy and being exasperated by talking to a laptop all day.

What my BSF was doing to me here was making me selfish and tricking me into thinking that Covid and its lockdowns were the problem. Yet everything that came with Covid was out of my control and getting upset and beleaguered with the limited way of living was completely pointless. More than that, I was really annoying the people I lived with! I am firmly signed up to the mindset of not wasting time and energy on the things that you can do nothing about, yet here I was being the epitome of everything I disagree with. That's how far my BSF had pulled me away from being my true self.

My BSF made me miss the things that being at home gave me, like not having to sit in traffic jams or shlep halfway across the country overnight to get to my next place of work. It also made me gloss over the opportunity it gave me every day to have breakfast with my daughters and spend my breaks and lunches in the garden with my wife, kids and cat. And when I finished work, I could get out of my chair and already be at home ready to have our tea together. I also completely took for granted the fact that I could still work when many others had that taken away from them.

Imagine 2020 being your second year in business!! Yet I still continued to work with new clients and engage with people from all around the world from my kitchen.

However, my BSF wouldn't allow me to see all of those positive things nor take any confidence from them. It completely persuaded me that I was going to be stuck at home forever and that the joy I get from being in a room with people had been taken away from me.

'They never did get it right
Since they got it so low.'

– OCEAN COLOUR SCENE

It took me until 2021 to realise what my BSF was doing to me during Covid times because Covid itself wasn't the problem. The problem was that I get my energy from people. I have an innate preference for extroversion and that's what was causing me so much pain and misery. It wasn't the restrictions placed on us that was really the problem for me. They were the same for everyone. It was only in 2021 when I started to get back out there and work with people in person that I saw the BS that my BSF had made me believe and blame on things that weren't going to change just because I wanted them to. My BSF has an on-off switch that is: -

- Working in isolation – BSF ON
- Working with other people – BSF OFF

Sure, I like my own company and I am good at staying motivated and getting the work done in a quiet space, but it has to be balanced with time in a room with people and the spontaneity and human connection that it brings. When I realised that working with other people being taken away from me was the real trigger for my negative emotions, I could choose a positive response to the accompanying thoughts and feelings. I chose the attitude I took towards it and behaved in a way that triggered positive emotions for me, even when I was spending all day talking to a laptop.

I changed my routine to include things that gave me a positive energy and started to run my own online events to bring like-minded people together so we could get through Covid together and replicate, as best I could, the buzz that I get from being with people. I took control from my BSF and showed myself that, even in the hardest times, I didn't have to follow the path set out for me by my BSF. Instead, I turned the rest of the pandemic into an opportunity to learn from my experiences and work hard at creating the opportunities that I wanted for myself once the world re-opened.

'Yeah, I learned in my time
That it's all a pantomime
You just need to be your friend
I'm alright
There's a beautiful light on the horizon.'

– LIAM GALLAGHER

Enjoy the moments that you work hard for

March 2022 was a month when I really lost my shit thanks to my BSF. This was the month before my first book was published. It should have been a month for me to really enjoy and bask in the glory of the hard work I had put in and the risk I had taken to write a book. I went into March 2022 with the manuscript all finished and with the publishers doing their bit towards getting it ready to go for the following month. We had agreed on the design of the book, which I absolutely loved, and really showed off my modernism and music-inspired branding. I had an online tour of events planned with places booked for me to promote the book and share with the world what they could expect from it. My in-person book launch was organised and the tickets were sold out.

Yet my BSF made me forget all of those positive things and made this month a living hell for me. It repeatedly told me that the book was shit and that I had made the biggest mistake of my life by believing that I could write a book that people would read. I started to chase my publisher before the deadlines were due and expected everything to go wrong. I got completely lost in the marketing and promotion of the book, which is something I do not enjoy. It made me forget to enjoy becoming a published author and that I was about to fulfil a lifelong ambition of mine. I came so close to pulling the plug on the whole thing and cancelling the book being published.

In the middle of a sleepless night, I sent an e-mail to my publisher telling them that I wasn't going to bother with the book launch and just ignore the book coming out because I didn't want anything to do with it! I was steadfast in my belief that I had written a load of shite and my BSF made me think that it would be funny to publish the book then quit my coaching business and just get a job where no-one could find me or know that I was an author!

What made me shut down my BSF this time was a conversation with someone who I implicitly trust (hello Aimee Bateman, you wonderful human being) and who I had asked to host my book launch event. We had a call planned to finalise plans for the event and Aimee had no idea that my intention for the call was to tell her that she was no longer needed for the event and that I was going to do it all myself before cancelling the thing completely.

I joined the call and Aimee told me how excited she was for the event and how much she loved the book having read my manuscript. I sat there on the call listening to Aimee, knowing that she wasn't blowing smoke up my arse and her positive feedback and encouragement was genuine. I opened up to Aimee about how I was feeling and she listened and reminded me that what I was going through was totally normal and that it was OK and told me to imagine how I was going to feel once the book was out there and people were reading it and sharing how much they enjoyed it. She also asked me about why I gave a shit if some people didn't like the book, giving me the kick up the arse that I needed by making me remember that I didn't want to be *"everyone's cup of tea"*; one of the strongest messages in the book was about not fitting in and doing things differently.

That conversation with Aimee empowered me to shut down my BSF and is an example of one of the key tactics that I employ to choose a positive response through talking things through with the people that I trust and have my best interests at heart. My BSF was making me internalise all of my natural worries, telling me that I was all alone and that my book would turn people against me. Which was such BS! Sometimes you need someone else to be your weapon of choice in shutting down your BSF.

'Hope that I will live my life with something soulful when I die.'

– PALACE

Do what brings you joy – your BSF hates that

Through all the years when my BSF was in full operation, one of the consistent things that it held me back from was choosing to do what I really wanted to do. It gave me the sense that the negativity I was living with was going to be around forever. It made me think that I should "stay in my lane" and that no-one would be interested in what I have to say or believe that I could help them be their best version of themselves. I told myself for years that the best thing that I could do with my career was to give up and join the legions of people who moan about their jobs and wait until someone else told me it was time for me to retire.

One of the biggest contributors towards winning my battles with my BSF was making the choice to do what brought me joy and to put myself out there. To not be afraid to fail and have a go at doing the things that are ambitious and need true commitment from me. Shutting down my BSF ignited the passion that I have for helping others to be the leader they want to be and work with their teams in the way they want to. I really believe that if you choose to go to work every day then you can choose to make it a positive experience for you and those around you. That really puts your BSF firmly in its place, when you choose to put that passion into action.

Whatever it is that fires your passion and brings you joy, your BSF will try to keep you as far away from it as possible. It hates joy and wants to envelope you in its blanket of pessimism and self-doubt. I know that my BSF detests me being able to have days when my attitudes and behaviours align with what I stand for as I help others to shut down their own BSF.

The "Work Wanker"

A great example of the power of shutting down your BSF is Andy, who was a 1-2-1 coaching client of mine. Andy and I worked together for 18 months and, when we first started out, his BSF was in full flow, making him doubt himself and question whether he could truly lead his team. Andy shared with me how he was being one of those leaders who tried to do everything and not let his team take responsibility. The thought of him giving them feedback or having honest conversations with them to set expectations frightened him. His BSF was holding him back from being his true, authentic self as a leader and impacted on his home life too. Andy shared with me how this was compounded by his wife asking him why he was being the "Work Wanker" who spent his nights on his laptop doing tasks that his team should be doing and sending out emails instead of being present at home with his family.

Andy and I worked on building his confidence through his emotional intelligence and enhancing his ability to make positive choices about how he worked so that he would be able to shut off from work once he finished for the day. He was taking on far too much, acting from fear rather than as the driven, motivated person he really was.

One of the things that filled me with joy when working with Andy was when he said, *"I used to be full of anxiety and worried that I was going to make a mistake. Now I go to work being clear on the value that I bring. I feel like I have gone back to being the person that I know I am."* I felt so much pride when Andy got in touch twelve months after we'd finished working together to tell me that he now had the confidence to apply for and get a job at a more senior leadership level.

'I've got my purpose back
I'm finally on my way.'

– STONE FOUNDATION

I take no credit for what Andy achieved. He did all the hard work whilst I supported him through coaching and challenging him to make positive choices. The joy I feel from seeing people make those positive choices and empowering themselves to shut down their BSF keeps me away from the comfort zone that my BSF wants to imprison me in. Andy shutting down his BSF helps me to shut down mine, and I know that will leave it muttering to itself and shrinking to its dark corner where it resides.

If you're struggling with your BSF, know that it CAN be different. You can be who you want to be and can do what brings you joy.

'It's my time to be here with you
I waited a long time to sing
this song to you
Many roads I had to travel on
Created my blues and the tears came too
It's your time, don't waste another day.'

– BOBBY HARDEN AND THE SOULFUL SAINTS

What have we done in this chapter?

- Experienced how the BSF can ruin your mental health
- Seen how close people can come to losing their battle with their BSF
- Recognised the importance of emotional intelligence and how it will save you from your BSF
- Reminded ourselves that we all have triggers that can switch on our BSF
- Set the tone for the hard work it takes to shut down your BSF
- Demonstrated how the BSF can drive you to make bad decisions
- Shown how we can make positive choices and fight back against our BSF

Coaching questions to get you thinking about shutting down your BSF...

- What does your BSF do to you?
- When has your emotional intelligence come to your rescue?

- What positive choices can you empower yourself to make?
- How well do you really know yourself?
- What brings you joy?
- Where can you see your BSF triggering you?

Mental Health Support

If you are struggling with your own mental health, there is a lot of support out there. Whilst I can only tell my own story, I understand that it is different for everyone and I am not trying to be a mental health expert. I choose to see my BSF as the instigator of my mental health because it helps me to win my daily battles with anxiety and depression.

Your emotional intelligence and ability to choose a positive response is ultimately what can help everyone to foster better mental health. There are some steps to take first, including seeking professional help to start the process of change through talking about it. **I have included details of mental health support that is out there at the end of the book.**

PART TWO

SHUTTING DOWN YOUR BSF

CHAPTER FOUR

HOW YOU CAN SHUT DOWN YOUR OWN BULLSHIT FACTORY

'Nobody can do everything
But everybody can do something.'

– STONE FOUNDATION

The time has now come for you to shut down your BSF. In this chapter, we're taking action. The first step in shutting it down is to work on you as an individual which I'll guide you through before demonstrating how I help leaders and teams to shut down their collective BSFs – remember that It Always Starts With You.

In this chapter, I will offer different techniques that all have the same principle at their heart: developing a lethal combination of your self-awareness and self-management. Those two combined are how you choose a positive response to the negative thoughts and feelings that your BSF produces. The more you choose a positive response to your thoughts and feelings, the more you will win your battle with your BSF. When you choose a positive response, you choose your attitudes and behaviours regardless of what BS your BSF starts with.

In this chapter I'll show you how to weave getting the upper hand over your BSF into your daily schedule so that choosing a positive response becomes the norm for you. I'll show you the ways you can build up your optimism and positivity to overcome your BSF. This is where your work and life stops being something that you don't enjoy to something that feels how you want it to feel. The key to shutting down your BSF is doing the work on yourself proactively. I want you to see shutting down your BSF as an ongoing process. The proactive work you do influences your own heart and mind so when the moment arrives that your BSF starts to fire up its production line, you are ready and fully prepared to choose a positive response.

This isn't about "taking a breath" or "counting to ten" when the emotions kick off, it is about choosing to work on yourself each day so you can build up your immunity to everything coming off the BSF production line. The work you do on yourself becomes your force field protecting you from your BSF. I will show you how to work on yourself so shutting down your BSF becomes second nature. As a bonus, you'll also start to fuel your thoughts and feelings with optimism. Even just reading this chapter will make your BSF uncomfortable; it will hate you for just starting to take action to tell it to "do one" and leave you alone to live your life feeling good about yourself.

All of the techniques I introduce you to are ones that I have done myself and come back to every day. I couldn't have gotten this far into writing the book without them! They brought me back from the brink when my BSF was telling me that this book is shit and a waste of time. I use these techniques with coaching clients and with teams. I have done these with all manner of people in all sorts of settings and they work for pent-up CEOs, senior leadership teams and the odd Neggy Nelly who resisted them at first.

One of the most powerful parts of my work is when I complete a 1-2-1 or Team Coaching programme and, months later, I catch up with clients who tell me that they are still using these techniques because of how impactful they have become. That's my dream for you – that you will still be using these techniques years after reading this book. This chapter will be the one you complete, put down and then pick up again when your BSF tries a different way of producing its BS. I will share some real examples and stories as we work through shutting down your BSF.

'Yeah, I feel better today
I think that shit was just a phase
My whole outlook's changed
I've even stopped feelin' strange.'

– THE TWANG

This is hard graft NOT a walk in the park

As a straight-talking Northerner, I can only be straight with you: shutting down your BSF is no simple task. You can't shut it down today and expect to wake up tomorrow with it completely gone. You must be prepared to put the hard graft in to build a solid foundation so that when the shit hits the fan, you've got the skills baked in to respond positively. All of the techniques I share here require conscious and consistent effort to become part of how you shut down your BSF every single day.

It's not easy to shut it down because the production line will run for as long as you live. Let's have a quick reminder of that production line so we're clear on what we're fighting when we use these techniques: -

1. It starts by producing some pretty uncomfortable thoughts and feelings.

2. This then moves on to producing negative self-talk, and you can be a right bastard to yourself.

3. Your pessimistic self-image comes next, making sure you don't think very much of yourself.

4. The penultimate stage produces a gloom-ridden anticipation of how things will go for you.

5. The end product of the BSF manufacturing process is... Reactive Attitudes and Behaviours, which are the products of your BSF. This is what everyone else sees.

Shutting it down isn't about being able to close down the factory and throw away the keys. It is about having the maximum self-awareness to recognise when it fires up again and understand why it is kicking back into action. Then you can trigger your self-management to stop it in its tracks. Using these techniques will give you that big red STOP button on the side of the production line which you can bash with your fist to halt it and move on to a positive production line where the products are in pristine condition and put a smile on your face.

When you start to shut down your BSF, you will probably be feeling pretty pleased with yourself; you will be starting to get one up on it, but you mustn't allow yourself to get complacent. Your BSF will try to resist you using these techniques. It will start another one of its dirty tricks campaigns to try to switch the negative production line back on. You can hit that red STOP button at any stage of the production. After a while, you will hit it as quickly as a quiz show contestant about to win a million pounds, but for now we just want to get into the habit of hitting it as soon as you spot the BSF firing up. Wherever your STOP button needs to be, you can always choose a positive response. Even if it is after your reactive attitudes and behaviours, you can still bash the STOP button and choose to never repeat them again.

Consistency will be key for you when you use these techniques to shut down your BSF because your BSF is exemplary when it comes to being consistent and you need to match that. It will pump out its BS for eternity and never even break into a sweat. The more consistent you are the harder it is for the BSF to see an opportunity to kick its negative production line into action as you take charge of your attitudes and how you behave. Your BSF will even show some resistance when you are physically doing these techniques. I'll share some painful examples from my own experience of it doing that to me! Your resistance has to be even stronger so you can shift the storm clouds and walk into the sunshine of a BS-free world.

'In a world full of pain
Why add to it?
When there's none left to blame
You gotta face up to it.'

– PAUL WELLER

It is because of that resistance that all of the techniques you will use include the "F word" that your BSF really hates – FUN. They are all done in a way that puts a smile on your face whilst doing them and I am going to introduce them to you and instruct you how to use them in a light and upbeat way. That gives you the organic benefit of fighting your BSF using an approach that instinctively combats its dour and dismal approach. I'm going to give you loads of "stuff" that you can use to throw a spanner in the workings of the BSF production line. We'll take it step-by-step so you can learn to walk before you outrun your BSF. We'll first do some **Quick Stuff** which is quick to learn and adopt daily. Then we'll dig into the Cool Stuff which superpowers your ability to choose a positive response.

We're taking a fun approach to these techniques because your BSF is negativity personified. We have to fight it with all the light-heartedness and positivity we can to organically make its defence weaker. This approach also means that you will look forward to shutting down your BSF rather than feeling like it is too much or just more stuff that you need to do. Your BSF wants you to have a bad time all the time so let's work together and have ourselves a good time all the time.

**'Moved by an action that
changes the pattern of things
Simple reactions that pass
people by on the wind
May your words go on forever
May your kindness show no measure
Keep on breathing your life into every
little thing.'**

– STONE FOUNDATION

Choose your Mindset to shut down your BSF

Before we dig into the specific techniques that shut down your BSF, I need you to adopt a way of thinking about the BS that comes from it. The techniques are not something you can just lift off the page and they solve all your problems. You have to "wrap them" with a mindset that means your techniques hit the sweet spot for you. You see, in order to shut down your BSF, you have to first believe that you can do it. You have to know, firstly, that you can shut it down and, secondly, that you'll do this by choosing a positive response to your thoughts and feelings.

It is a mindset that requires you to go against two natural things that your BSF triggers: -

- **Resistance** – your BSF wants to pick a fight with you every day. It wants you to do the human thing and resist your emotions and try to "take the emotion out of it".
- **Judge yourself** – as if the initial BS isn't enough of a blow, your BSF has a secondary line of attack: judgement. It wants you to blame yourself for all that is bad in your world and carry around your self-judgement.

To successfully shut down your BSF, your mindset needs to be one that chooses to respond not resist and ditches the judgement. I will introduce both of these ways of thinking to you and then give you a technique to get you started.

Respond not resist

Your BSF hates being called out for what it is, it works best in the dark shadows so noticing when it fires up is a superpower. To do that effectively, you have to switch from resisting it to responding to it. Resistance is futile when it comes to your BSF. A natural reaction to a negative emotion is to try to resist it, to push back and try to fight it. This is a waste of time. The more you resist it, the stronger that emotion will become. Your BSF loves a good scrap and, when you try to resist the negativity that it fills your heart and mind with, the more intense it will become. When I was consumed by my BSF, I would fight my anxiety so hard and try to resist it by pushing back against it by continually wishing that I didn't feel that way and believing that just wishing for it to change would be enough. This would only make me even more anxious because I would then be anxious about feeling anxious and even more anxious about not being able to stop feeling anxious! It really is like being on the proverbial shit-covered hamster wheel.

You can't make an emotion disappear. They are going to come whether you like it or not. Especially the negative ones from your BSF. The opportunity to shut down your BSF comes from recognising your emotions, understanding what is causing them and the thoughts and feelings that come with them, accepting them and then choosing a positive response to them. See your thoughts and feelings for what they are – just thoughts and feelings; they are NOT always reality. You do not have to do everything they tell you to do. A good way that I have learnt to deal with my thoughts and feelings is: -

1. Recognise them
2. Acknowledge them
3. Understand them
4. Choose how to positively respond to them
5. Get on with the rest of my life

A big part of me becoming confident in shutting down my BSF was being able to see my thoughts and feelings for what they were – just that. They are thoughts and feelings; they are not real. Particularly with anxiety, I learnt to see it for exactly what it is: an intangible thought passing through my mind. I don't need to react to it or try to fight it, just allow it to pass on by and get on with my day.

Your thoughts and feelings are a big part of the shared human existence. Your BSF wants you to live a lonely existence whilst making you believe that you are the only one with negative thoughts and feelings. You are never the only one so do not allow your BSF to make you believe that. The people you have been on a Teams call with today have negative thoughts and feelings. The person next to you on the train or in the gym or in the queue for coffee also has them. And that is OK. Empathise with yourself and focus on positively responding to them rather than trying to fight them and wishing you didn't have them.

A lot of my coaching clients say things like *"How do I stop feeling like this?"* or *"I just want to stop thinking that"*, and my answer is always the same – *"You can't. All you can do is choose how to respond."*

**'You're not alone you know, you're not alone you know
You're not alone at all.'**

– THE ENEMY

Ditch the Judgement

When I started to shift from "Old Tim" to "New Tim" and began shutting down my BSF, one of the first things I did was start to empathise with myself. "Old Tim" would not only have the BS to deal with but it was also wrapped in a second layer of shit – all the guilt I'd felt for experiencing the BS.

My BSF would leave me feeling useless, which then made me judge myself for feeling useless, which led to constant guilt for feeling useless because I had no real reason to, especially when *"I am better off than most people"* so how dare I feel that way? This judgement makes it hard to see the BS for what it is because it twists it in your heart and mind so not only are you dealing with the initial negativity but you are also having to contend with the self-judgement for thinking and feeling that way in the first place.

"New Tim" still had the same initial thoughts and feelings, but I stopped blaming myself for the negativity coming from my BSF and instead reminded myself *"It's OK, you are human"*. A good example of this is when I first started working for myself and would do a piece of work for the first time. My BSF would fire up telling me that I am not worthy of the work and that I am going to mess it up. I would step in and choose a positive response which started with me reminding myself that I am only human and then going in hard on my BSF by being specific for understanding why I was thinking and feeling that way (i.e. *"You are going to feel nervous – you have never done this before and it is really important to you"*). This practice of positively responding instead of going down the judgement rabbit hole meant I could accept my natural thoughts and feelings for the BS they are and move on without any lingering sense of negativity or guilt. Ditching the judgement gave me much brighter days and meant that I no longer lost time and energy trying to fight my emotions and instead could now choose a positive response to whatever my BSF could throw at me.

Don't judge yourself on or because of your emotions. Remain curious and open-minded about why you have your thoughts and feelings. Instead of judging and thinking *"I shouldn't be feeling like this"*, be brave. Stop yourself from buying into your emotions by freeing yourself from your own judgements and be open-minded about what you can achieve. One of the bravest things you can do is just sit with your negative thoughts and feelings and not judge yourself or what you can or can't do as a result of them. Feeling and thinking about something is very different to *being* something. There are days when I feel like a useless dad but just because I feel that doesn't mean it is actually true. Your BSF can be very persuasive and make you think that its BS is the gospel truth. Remember – it's not you and neither is it me – it is your BSF. When you stop judging yourself on your emotions, it stops you from turning that emotion into criticism.

'How much more are we
supposed to tolerate?
Can't you see there's more
to me than my mistakes
Sometimes I get this feeling
– makes me hesitate.'

– MICHAEL KIWANUKA

Try this Five Year Activity

Here is an activity to help you to stop and think about what is possible for you and be curious about what the future can hold for you. Move away from the BSF thoughts and feelings telling you that you are not good enough and move into reality by being curious and opening your mind to what is possible. I use this with coaching clients who are stuck in their negative emotions and are starting to believe the BS is the truth. It is a good demonstration of you purposely stopping to choose a positive response and ditch the judgement.

Go back five years in your mind and write down what your BSF was saying to you then. Then remind yourself of what you have still achieved in those five years.

Now go five years into the future in your mind and write down what you will be able to say to yourself about what you have achieved in those next five years.

When I do this and go back five years, I see the negative BS that was being produced by my BSF and I can see things that I never knew were possible until I stopped resisting my BSF and ditched the self-judgement. I opened my own mind up to the possibility of them happening. Five years ago, I never knew: -

- I could write a book.
- I would successfully work for myself.

- I could stand on stage and confidently engage hundreds of people.

You must remember that we are all always a work in progress. No-one has it all sussed and we're all making it up as we go along because none of us have ever lived our tomorrow yet. There is always so much more we can do and so much we can learn about ourselves. This becomes possible through stopping judging ourselves based on our thoughts and feelings and choosing a positive response to believe what is possible.

'Don't judge yourself on your thoughts and feelings Judge yourself on how you choose to respond.'

The Quick Stuff

Let's get you shutting down your BSF off to a strong start with the daily techniques you can start doing right now. These techniques will help you to get your days off to a good start. They will give you constant self-awareness and the fuel you need to self-manage both proactively and in the moment. It is these techniques that made me go from doing my best Charlie Brown impression, walking into work with a rain cloud above my head, to having a spring in my step that meant I confidently swaggered into work like Liam Gallagher about to headline Wembley.

I do need to make clear at this point that the Quick Stuff ideas are not "quick wins". There is no such thing as a quick win when shutting down your BSF. They are quick to pick up – you can start doing them before you finish this chapter. The key is doing the quick stuff consistently to give you a daily boost for winning the battle with your BSF. And to help with that consistently, each technique here has a music theme to help them keep spinning like your favourite records in your mind and give you that constant beat of positivity and optimism to drown out the dull sounds of negativity and pessimism that come from your BSF. These techniques will give you that feeling you get when you put your favourite song on the jukebox to replace the crap that someone else is playing and everyone else in the pub shows their appreciation. Only it will be you appreciating you and your positive choices.

'All that's lost can still be found
You're too good for giving up.'

– LIAM GALLAGHER

1. *Your Fighting Talk*

What is it?

To choose to shut down your BSF every day, you need to talk to yourself when you sense it kicking off. In particular, talk to yourself in a way that is authentically you. When the BSF fires up, the risk is that it takes over the microphone in your head and screams mean propaganda at you. It turns your internal monologue into the moaning bastard at work who tells anyone in earshot what they think about something that no-one else cares about. Or the loud drunk in the pub who talks over everyone else, interrupting your conversations to tell you something completely irrelevant and constantly changing the subject. Your Fighting Talk is how you grab the mic back and shut down the moaners and pervasive drunks.

This technique is a way of taking your negative inner monologue and turning it into positive inner dialogue. It is like having the power to always respond with a good comeback. You know, it is like in the movies when the hero says something back to the bully that completely shuts them down. Only, it's not for a one-off scene in your life, it is for every single day. Whether it is to fight a bout of imposter syndrome or to just repel the BS telling you that today is a bad day, you have to strike back quickly with your Fighting Talk to make sure your BSF doesn't take over your self-talk and evolves it into a negative self-image. When my BSF grabs the mic inside my head, I need my Fighting Talk to rescue me and hand the mic back to me so I can respond to the BS propaganda and leave the moaners and annoying drunks behind.

What are the benefits?

Remember that your BSF grabs that mic in your mind and chats a load of pretty convincing BS. When you choose to have a positive conversation with yourself, it makes it much harder for the BSF to grab that mic. This technique means you can play out one of those many scenes from films where the corporate tosser is ruining people's lives and then finally someone stands up to them, calls out their BS and says it like it is to escape from the dreary existence that someone else is imposing on them. The most important person that you'll ever have a conversation with is yourself and this technique makes those inner conversations ones that you buzz off and want to keep having.

What happens if I don't do it?

"Old Tim" was rubbish at doing this and I would buy in to every thought and every feeling that came from my BSF. This would see me lose days at work just stuck in the funk of my BSF as I believed its BS and would either lose my rag with other people or completely retreat into my shell,

"The most important person that you'll ever have a conversation with is yourself" beating myself up, expecting every meeting to go badly and treating every e-mail like a personal attack on me and my work. These were the days when I would feel stressed and lost, aching for a different experience but doing nothing about it. My imposter syndrome would turn into ostrich syndrome and, without my Fighting Talk, I would bury my head firmly in the sand whilst my BSF ruled by self-talk.

"New Tim" made a choice. I chose to recognise the BS thoughts and feelings coming from my BSF and I started to respond and say to myself, *"OK that's my BSF talking. I don't want to think or feel this way. I want to think and feel..."* I used that to trigger me into fighting back and shutting down my BSF. This response makes me take action and positively respond to my BSF. Even on the days when my anxiety is playing up, I use this response and keep talking to myself to show my BSF that it can't take control and that I will fight back.

'Gotta leave that nine
to five upon the shelf
An' just enjoy yourself
Step on and groove.'

– MICHAEL JACKSON

What do I need to do?

You need to write your own script for what is going on in your mind. The BSF will start the conversation and talk to you through your negative thoughts and feelings and BS self-talk. That's OK – you can't stop that. What you need to do is choose how to respond to it. Imagine your bad days when your BSF is kicking off and your head is full of its BS. Now imagine what you want to say to it, in the way that you speak, that will have maximum impact in shutting it up and giving you back control for how you think and feel. Some examples that my coaching clients use to consider and rewrite for themselves are: -

"Stop. That's not me."

"Oh, just fuck off will you. That's not what I think."

"Right. Let's take a beat."

"Piss off, bugger lugs. I am in charge here."

"I'm not going down that road."

"Ha ha whatever nobhead."

This is the first step, to get in your strong response that then opens the dialogue up for what you want to say to yourself next. You can see that some are more direct than others. You have to choose what works for you. My Fighting Talk of *"OK that's my BSF talking. I don't want to think or feel this way. I want to think and feel..."* isn't exactly tough-talking but it resonates with me because it reminds me that it is my BSF being negative not me and I then follow it up with the context in which my BSF is trying to enjoy itself and I then lead the conversation with myself to turn the BS into optimism for what is going to happen next. You need to choose your Fighting Talk and make it part of your daily vocabulary, even practising it and reminding yourself that it is there for you. I use mine proactively to consider what might go wrong and remind myself that if anything bad happens then I will use my Fighting Talk to choose how to respond to it. I will not get caught up in the negativity, instead I will tell myself how I want to think and feel. This has been huge for me and helped me to fight my BSF when bad things happen, ranging from my train getting cancelled or a client ghosting me, and trigger the BS.

Successfully shutting the BSF down

I worked with a leadership team helping them to develop their emotional intelligence. A big part of this was showing them how to shut down their BSF and coaching them to choose a positive response to their negative thoughts and feelings. One of the leaders, Megan, took this on when she was faced with a nervous and gloomy anticipation of what her days were going to entail. At the start of one of her sessions, Megan approached me excitedly and proclaimed, *"It works, Tim. It really works"*. I asked Megan to explain to me what she meant, and she told me how the previous week she had travelled to London to present to a customer and she was full of nerves, expecting the customer to give her a hard time.

Megan explained that, as she was coming up on the escalator in the tube station just before she got to the customer's office, she was overwhelmed with nerves and started to dread the meeting. It was at this point that she spoke to herself saying, *"It's just my Bullshit Factory,"* which then cleared the path for her to tell herself that the meeting was going to go well, reminding herself how much she really wanted to be in London to deliver her presentation.

Megan went on to explain how telling herself *"It's just my Bullshit Factory"* completely changed her experience that day and, through choosing a positive response, she shifted herself away from the negative thoughts and feelings and instead boosted her confidence. This meant that she nailed the presentation and the customer meeting was a huge success. Megan told me how doing this made her feel like she had removed a black cloud hanging over her that day and enabled her to get into the right headspace to walk into her customer meeting full of confidence and expecting it to go well.

Make that one of the first steps you take to shutting down your BSF. Choose what you will say to yourself when it starts to fire up and you can call out its BS before putting yourself back on track for being yourself and having a positive experience.

What will your Fighting Talk be to respond to your BSF with?

'I'll do it all day if it feels good
Don't bring your bullshit to my party.'

– THE RECORD COMPANY

2. Your Playlists

What is it?

The quickest of the quick stuff. You could literally do this whilst reading this chapter. This is a technique that rolls over your subconsciousness and blocks the radio waves from your BSF so you are inspired by sounds that mean something to you. When put into practice, it is your way of shutting out the BS of the world and putting you at the centre of your universe so you can face every day the way you want to. It means you can choose the soundtrack of your life by turning down the volume of your BSF and instead blasting into your heart and mind what you really want to think and feel.

What are the benefits?

Your playlists shut down your BSF by proving to it that you are your own DJ. Whilst this technique is one to practise consistently every day, it is also one that brings instant benefits to you. Think about those times when you come off a shitty call or out of a boring meeting. Your playlists will instantly lift your mood after those negative experiences and set you on the right track for leaving the BS of calls and meetings behind. You own the decks in your heart and mind. It might want to grind you down with feelings of misery and despair, but you can fight back with songs that put a spring in your step and get you strutting your stuff.

Your playlists use music to flood your heart and mind with inspirational things that take over how you think and feel about yourself. It is like having a party in your heart and mind that your BSF is not invited to. In fact, it is outside getting a good kicking off the bouncers because it tried to jump the queue and was rude and aggressive. So, your playlist bouncers took action and sorted it out. All the while, you're inside having the time of your life and feeling like you can face anything that today throws at you.

Music cuts through the BS in your mind and goes straight to your heart, releasing positive emotions to use in the fight against your BSF. Music moves you. It makes you want to dance and live a happy life. Music is there for us no matter what the day is like; it is a primal force that we have used for years to turn our experiences into positive ones. Music has changed the world for more than a hundred years now and your playlists will show you how to use your music to change your world.

I have loved music since Oasis took over the world in 1995 and am totally obsessed with it. It fires so much passion in me and I have an unlimited number of songs and albums that take me back to a happy time, to a gig I went to with my mates or to a time in my life when an album completely took over my consciousness. Some of that goes back to my youth and feeling free and some of it also goes back to my depressive years and the songs and albums that helped to get me through. David Bowie isn't just one of the greatest artists of all time, he literally saved me from my suicidal thoughts so many times.

'Who needs TV
When you've got T-Rex?'

– MOTT THE HOOPLE

Think about those times when a song comes on the radio or in a pub or the DJ puts it on at a wedding and you have to get up and dance to it whilst exclaiming *"I love this song, I haven't heard it for ages,"* before singing along to every single word. Well, when you use your playlists to shut down your BSF, you can have that feeling ten-fold every single day.

What happens if I don't do it?

Your subconscious mind will be full of BS. A combination of the world's BS and the BS from your BSF. Believe me when I say that is not a good place to be. "Old Tim" was there for years. I would leave the house to go to work with a head full of BS. The chances are that I would have woken up with my BSF production line off and running and would have dragged myself out of bed looking like "Sadness" from *Inside Out* as I trudged to the bathroom and got myself ready for another day of BSF-induced dreariness. As if that wasn't bad enough, I followed that by eating my Frosties whilst watching *BBC News*. I'd get in my car and put on the same BS radio show that played the same BS songs every day, often in the vain hope that I got the call to win their BS listener competition. To make it even worse for myself, I would then stop at the shop on the way to work and buy a tabloid newspaper, which is basically BS that you can hold in your hands.

The days when I was giving myself a double helping of BS are the ones that I never want to go back to. That mix of what my BSF was producing and lapping up the BS of the world was toxic for me and made me be someone that I am not – pessimistic, opinionated without having a real opinion and distracted by nonsense that didn't concern me and wasn't under my control. Sound like anyone you work with?!

The "New Tim" part of this technique is more of a "went back to real Tim" story as I chose to stop losing so much time and energy to BS and instead created and blasted out my own playlists on my way to work to show up as my true, authentic self. I wouldn't be the me consumed with BS, I would be the me who is obsessed with good music and intends to have a good time at work whilst helping others to do the same.

This change first started back when I worked for a company whose culture was testing to say the least. I was part of an L&D Team whose M.O. seemed to be *"Moan as much as you can. Give them death by PowerPoint and hope they don't ask any questions"*. "New Tim" decided to choose a positive response and not be like the BSF-battered whinging bastards who surrounded me. I made sure that whenever I was facilitating, the day always started in the training room with my tunes playing to get me in the mood and help me to overcome my nerves. The tunes stayed on as the participants arrived and were played as they worked in groups to add some atmosphere to the room.

It's a practice that I still follow today and still brings me joy every time I facilitate a workshop or event. I see the impact this has on people as they either comment in an appreciative way that *"Ooh we don't normally have music on"* or they tell me how much they love one of the tunes that comes on and it helps us to strike up a conversation. That way I can find common ground with people I have just met and need to build trust with. My playlists give me a force-field-like feeling for battling my BSF as I fight the nerves and fear of facilitating a room of strangers with my favourite tunes playing.

A quick sidenote to encourage you to shut down your BSF with your playlists – you might think that "Old Tim's" experiences were bad enough but I am going back to the pre-social media days so imagine how much damage this does to people nowadays when they don't choose their playlists? They fill their days with a head full of comparison and algorithm-driven BS. Give me a playlist of tunes to sing my heart out to over that drivel any day of the week. I have chosen to turn my smartphone into a jukebox in my arse pocket so, instead of all the "Influencer" BS notifications, my screen only lights up with the next inspirational tune starting up.

''Cause music is the mantra
Unwinding your head
Music is the question
To things unsaid.'

– RICHARD ASHCROFT

What do I need to do?

I am going to break this down into three steps for you: -

Step One – Stop and think about the music that inspires you

When I say "inspires you", I mean the tunes that spark an urge within you to feel or do something positive. That is what "inspire" means. It doesn't need to be about someone winning the Olympics or a miraculous story about resilience or personal success. I mean the things that are personal to you and spark that inspiration in you. The music that inspires you comes from two things: 1) Your experiences and 2) Your taste in music!

Reflect now on the big moments in your life – your earliest memories. Your teenage years. The music being played in the pubs and clubs of your young adult life. A song that was playing when you first fell in love. Your first song at your wedding. Songs played at funerals. Songs from your favourite films. The songs that you have seen your favourite bands play live. The songs you were listening to when your kids were born. Songs that were there for you when you were down and going through bad times.

'Now this song is about you.'

– THE ENEMY

We all have those songs that have soundtracked our lives. When you read that last paragraph, your mind will have been coming to life with vivid memories. It was probably taking you back to the music that your mum and dad used to play (hello Roxy Music and Meat Loaf). Or those rebellious teenage times when you play the music that your mum and dad wouldn't like (Nirvana and Pearl Jam CDs blasting out of my bedroom). Or maybe you went back to your young adult life when you were first beginning to understand who you really are and choose your own path in life (I now have Ocean Colour Scene on the record player in my mind). Whatever experiences you have that are linked to music are personal to you. The experience can be whatever you want it to be, and the music is whatever was playing during or around that experience. Bring them back into your mind now.

Your taste in music is the bleeding obvious part of this. Your playlists have to be YOURS. Not what Spotify or Apple Music put on the latest "You might like" list or whatever manufactured pop star YouTube is promoting today. You choose what goes on your playlists based on your taste in music. Some clients I have helped to create playlists apologise to me when telling me that they have made one of 80s pop songs or ones of their favourite Jungle tracks. The only things that need to be in your playlists are the things that spark positive memories in you. They take you away from your mundane need for survival and the risk-averse fun police of your BSF. It doesn't matter what goes on there;

it is personal to you. I don't care what is on your playlists. I only care that they inspire you to shut down your BSF.

'May the good Lord shine a light on you
Make every song your favourite tune
May the good Lord shine a light on you
Warm like the evening sun.'

– THE ROLLING STONES

Step Two – Create your playlists

This is the practical bit where you need to get up off your arse and do something, or at least pick up the jukebox that is your smartphone and create your playlists. This is the only part of the book that might cost you a few bob as you might need to subscribe to a music streaming platform so you can enjoy your playlists ad-free. However, if you're one of the really cool kids who has got back into cassettes then you could make a mixtape instead!

It really is that simple – make good use of the technology that is there at your fingertips. You might need to go back to basics and write down your music-inspired memories or write down your favourite bands, albums and songs to spark your inspiration and make it easier to search through the millions of songs available on your digital devices.

My playlists include some dedicated to my favourite artists or genres. I have playlists for Weller, Arcade Fire, Bowie, DMA's and The Beatles. And I have ones for Soul and R&B and 90s Indie. I even have a guilty pleasure Dance Tunes playlist for when I want to forget the BS and go back to part of my misspent youth. I have a playlist that I listen to when writing which is a massive mix of my favourite tunes plus the oddities that you pick up along the way. It ranges over 80 years of music, from 1950s rock 'n' roll to Wham!, and is two full days long in duration!

Put the book down and create your first one now. Have some fun doing it and watch as a big smile adorns your face as the tunes take you back to a happy place. Or they might even make you get up and dance or get up and sing. They will definitely move you. When you come back to the book, you can have them playing whilst you continue to shut down your BSF.

'Get up and dance
Get up and smile
Get up and drink to the days
Who are gone in the shortest while.'

– OCEAN COLOUR SCENE

Step Three – Listen to your playlists

Creating your playlists is not where this ends. You must choose to listen to them at the right time for you. You can listen to them when getting ready for work or preparing for your first Teams call of the day. They will definitely fire you up for that big meeting or presentation. They are a great antidote to the shitty meeting that you have just sat through. You can't beat driving home from work or sitting on the train with your headphones on and your playlists playing whilst everyone else appears lost in a world of bad days and hopelessness. Be practical here; look in your calendar to see the times in the days ahead when you are likely to need an instant boost from your playlists. There is always a time to listen to your playlists and be inspired to shut down your BSF. You must choose when the time is right for you.

For me, this means always listening to them as I drive to work with clients or before I go on a call. The first time you meet me, chances are that I have just been belting out "Shout to The Top" by the Style Council or another tune to get me in the right, positive frame of mind for what you need from me. When I am setting up the training room is a prime example of when my playlists help me. This time can be preceded by an exchange with a less than welcoming receptionist(!!) or by being shown into a room that instantly causes me some consternation in terms of size, layout or when I get told the infamous words: *"Don't put Blu Tack on the walls"*.

Despite how much I love my job, this final time before facilitating a workshop can be nerve-wracking and quite stressful for me. I want to get in the zone and get everything ready but it comes with many distractions. From the room issues to the client who wants to tell me all about their problems whilst I am setting up for the day or the participant who arrives early and either wants small talk or to tell me about the leadership workshops they have done before and how bad they were, there are plenty of potential stressors.

All of this contributes to my BSF firing up at the time when I least expect it. So, the first thing I do when I get into the room is connect to my speaker and blast out whatever playlist I need filtering into my consciousness that day. This takes me away from whichever distraction comes my way and allows me to remind myself that everything will be OK. At the end of the day, my journey home is filled with my playlists to stop my BSF from telling me that I did a bad job and to remind myself that the only thing that matters is that my attitudes and behaviours live up to what I stand for.

You might be thinking at this point *"It's just music, mate. How does that actually help me?"*. Well, that's exactly what your BSF wants you to think! It's not the music specifically that really makes the difference to you, it is you consistently making a positive choice for what goes into your heart and mind. The more you show your BSF that you will switch off the doom of the news and not get lost in the BS of social media, the more it starts to feel like there is no point in it striking up the production line because your tunes will instantly shut it down. That's where your playlists really pay dividends for you. It's not just as a proactive, daily habit to raise your optimism and fill your heart and mind with positivity. In those moments when other people and things start to awaken your BSF and the production line begins to stir, your playlists can shut it down for you and quickly move you back to being what you want to be – YOU.

Why be another one of those idiots who rely on a radio DJ to play a track that inspires you? Stick some on right now whilst you read the rest of this chapter. Let it wash over you and fill you with joy and confidence as you give your BSF the V's like you're on stage headlining Glastonbury.

'Once the music gets in you,
it doesn't leave you.'

– LIAM GALLAGHER

Successfully shutting the BSF down

"In between picking up dog poo, I am doing my e-mails," was the response from Jenny, a coaching client who I worked with over two years as she moved into her first exec role by joining a new organisation. Jenny is super experienced,

has years of leadership experience and is a well-connected expert in her specialist area. Yet when I met her, Jenny was riddled with self-doubt and had lost her purpose and, in her own words, was now experiencing her *"first ever crisis of confidence"*. Whilst Jenny was more than capable in her exec role and was performing well, her confidence took a hit due to the culture of her new organisation and making the transition from where she worked previously, where she knew everyone and had long-standing relationships.

Jenny and I did a lot of work on building up her confidence by enabling her to go back to being her true, authentic self and building her new relationships through honest conversations and building trust and rapport. The *"dog poo"* response came when I asked Jenny about her morning routine, which was prompted by her telling me that she is a morning person and wanted to do our sessions in the morning. The *"Morning Jenny"* I met at her first few sessions was not someone who you would describe as a morning person and was often fraught with anxiety and was clearly distracted by her own thoughts and feelings. She was often moving quite frantically and quickly shifting our conversation from topic to topic without any real rhyme or reason.

When I raised the subject of Jenny's morning routine, what she told me suggested she should be in a good headspace and relaxed when I met her as she described how her early mornings were either filled with gym workouts or walking her dog. There were no rushed school runs or oversleeping to make her late for work. I asked Jenny what she was listening to during her gym visits and dog walks and she told me that she listens to nothing and couldn't tell me what was on the TVs in the gym as she was always distracted by her self-talk overthinking and telling her that she needs to prove herself in her new role. When on her dog walks, she is distracted by doing her e-mails at 6:30am (in between picking up dog poo!).

I introduced the idea of playlists and asked Jenny to write down her top ten songs that inspire her and bring back positive memories for her. After she did that I asked her how she could make sure that she chooses to listen to them every morning. I went directly into reminding her that dog walks and gym workouts are prime times to shut out the BS and fill your heart and mind with good vibes ready for the day ahead.

Jenny set up her first playlist and, at her next session, her morning demeanour was transformed. She took great joy telling me how she had spent the morning *"bopping away to some Joy Division and Whitney Houston"* (an eclectic mix if ever there was one!) and how this had stopped her doing her e-mails and instead made her think about what she was doing at the weekend and how excited she was about it. This meant she turned up for work with her confidence turned up to the max and without any negative overthinking tainting her self-talk.

That's the power of choosing to listen to your playlist and shutting out the BS from your BSF and the wider world. It might seem like such a simple technique – and it is. That is the beauty of it. Doing something simple that gives you positive emotions shuts down your BSF and shows it that you are in control and know how to switch on your optimism and positivity. Your playlists clear your mind to focus on what is really important to you, and they are there for you, whenever you need them.

What needs to be on your playlists and when do you need to listen to them?

'Believe you can achieve it
Believe you can achieve it
Believe you can achieve it
Believing all the time.'

– SKYLIGHTS

Check out the playlist that I have created for you on Spotify that includes all of the songs whose lyrics inspire you throughout. Scan the QR code to access it.

3. Your Daily Mantras

What is it?

A technique that not nearly enough people practise. Your Daily Mantras are the things you want to tell yourself every day. This is a way of consistently being aware that you don't have to do everything your thoughts and feelings tell you to do. It takes you away from the heavy burden of anticipation that your BSF fills your heart and mind with. It is how you get on the front foot every day to choose a positive response to your BSF and shut it down. Many of us experience those thoughts and feelings that tell us today is going to be a bad day or that we should expect the worst to happen. When you choose to say your Daily Mantras to yourself, you turn those negative thoughts and feelings into what you want to hear about your day ahead. It is a conscious habit to adopt that infiltrates your subconsciousness, switching off the BSF production line so the only thing you produce are the emotions that make you feel good about yourself and ready to take on the world.

What are the benefits?

A good way to look at how this technique benefits you is to imagine how your favourite band gets introduced before they headline a festival. The anticipation has been building and the band's songs are playing over the speakers as the stage is prepared by their roadies and engineers. The sun is shining, you're with your mates and you know that this is going to be a great moment. The volume on the speakers starts to go down, the stage lights are dimmed, the crowd cheers and then the MC comes over the Tannoy to introduce them. That MC is never going to ruin your experience of that gig by telling the crowd, *"Put your hands together for a shit band who are about to play the worst gig you have ever been to which will completely ruin your day."* Of course, they don't! They tell you how amazing the band are and that you are about to have the time of your lives.

Yet, how many times do we tell ourselves something that ruins our anticipation of what is going to happen and makes us sleepwalk into days that get ruined by our thoughts and feelings. Now, going to work doesn't need to feel like the best gig you ever went to but we all at least want to have good days at work. We want to work with people with whom we share mutual respect, and we want the MC in our own hearts and minds to tell us that we're about to have a good day.

Your Daily Mantras make you feel the same about your days as you do about your music collection or your favourite album. If you were to ask me about my vinyl collection, I wouldn't tell you *"It's OK"* or be all coy in case you don't like some of my records. I will eulogise about it and tell you about the effort I went to to get some of my prize records. I will tell you about my favourite bands, whose LPs I have collected over years, and why some are more treasured than others. I will tell you that my record collection is the best fucking record collection in the world. You would do exactly the same when I ask you about your music collection or favourite artist or album or song. You would tell me in superlatives about why they are the best and why you love them and create a positive anticipation in me for listening to the music you are talking about.

Your Daily Mantras will do exactly the same for you. They will become your very own MC hyping you up by telling you that your day ahead will be one of the best fucking days you've ever had. They will trigger positive emotions in you like you are about to see your favourite band headline a festival. In the sun. With your mates. They will make you savour it and make you super defensive about having a good day. You won't allow any other BS to stop you thinking and feeling that way.

When you choose your Daily Mantras, you shift your perceptions from one of storm clouds gathering above you to clear, bright sunshine lighting the way for you to have the days you want to have. Your BSF can make you feel like you are carrying a ball and chain around with you, weighing you down so much that you drudge through your days consumed with negative thoughts and feelings telling you that today will be *"same old shit, different day"*.

You can choose to not be part of the *"same old shit"* brigade and instead benefit from telling yourself every day the things that you need to remember about yourself and what you want to anticipate for the day ahead. Practising your Daily Mantras makes the anxiety subside and you can move the BS out of the way. No-ones *wants* to have bad days but your BSF will bring them in abundance. Your Daily Mantras benefit you by putting you in control of how you think and feel about your days ahead. They also enable you to positively respond in the moment. Whilst they can't guarantee that you will have a good day, they do guarantee that you can start your days on the right footing and positively respond to whatever BS your days throw at you.

Your Daily Mantras get you off to a good start no matter what your BSF wakes you up with. So often, we start days in a shit mood so we only see the shit, but that allows the rest of our day to slowly transform into shit too. The self-fulfilling prophecy of telling ourselves we will have a bad day and so we have a bad day is one of your BSF's specialties; it wants you to tell yourself that every day. A major faulty product of your BSF is confirmation bias and it loves to articulate your self-talk so it tells you that you are about to have a bad experience. When your BSF gives you confirmation bias, it is negative and makes you reactive and likely to explode at any moment. Your BSF is what makes you catastrophise and turn a small problem into a massive, insurmountable problem.

Your BSF gives you your own Richter Scale inside of your head, making you decide how big of a problem it is. If your BSF is telling you that today will be a bad day then running into a traffic jam is enough to move you up to a feeling that your day is now going to be a disaster. It loves nothing more than shifting you to extreme disaster just because your first Teams call ran over and now you're flying into a rage before joining your next call. Both traffic jams and meetings overrunning are insignificant things, "First World Problems" if you will, but your BSF will shift your Richter Scale towards making them feel like molten lava is raining down on you and ruining the entire landscape of your day.

Your Daily Mantras shift the dial on your Richter Scale and help you to see things clearly, meaning the traffic jam is no more than an anomaly and the overrunning Teams call is nothing more than an incident. One that doesn't ruin the rest of your day. Using your Daily Mantras is a "double bubble" when it comes to the benefits you get as they set you up for a good day, so you have positive emotions about what is going to happen and feel in control and confident. Just stop and go back in your mind to the days when you expected that you were going to have a good day and recall how positive you felt and how confident that feeling made you. Your Daily Mantras can make you feel that way every day.

The second benefit relates to how it makes you able to positively respond in the moment. When something occurs that your BSF wants you to push up to level 10 on your Richter Scale, it now makes you feel neutral at best. Because your Daily Mantras become anchored in your subconscious mind, when shit happens, your subconscious mind kicks in to remind you how you wanted to think and feel during today. If you have allowed your BSF to tell you that today is going to be bad then, when something does happen, your subconscious mind tells you *"See, I knew today was going to be shit!"* and you are soon catastrophising over someone drinking the last of the milk from the work fridge. With your Daily Mantras kicking in from your subconscious mind, you can make a big problem into a small one by positively responding based on having told yourself that this day would go well. You can then put in reserve how you want to respond to the shit that the BSF throws at you.

Your Daily Mantras are a strong way to always remember that you are not your thoughts – you are your choices.

'I don't care how long this lasts
We have no future, we have no past
I write this now while I'm in control
I'll choose the words and
how the melody goes.'

– PAUL WELLER

What happens if I don't do it?

I am particularly well placed to answer that for you. "Old Tim" was a nightmare for letting his BSF tell him what his days were going to be like. I would storm into work ready for war even though all I was going to do was go to some meetings and have some 1-2-1's with my team. Those meetings would be treated like a personal affront as people asked me to give updates on what my team and I were working on. I would jump down people's throats with my answers like I was getting in the first blow, or I would get so consumed in the negativity coursing through my veins that I would be completely withdrawn, hardly speaking and never contributing to group discussions.

My BSF turned me into being so antagonistic that I would go into 1-2-1's with my team already convinced that it was a waste of time and that they wouldn't have done anything since last time. My team would often stay silent as I turned them into a one-way monologue driven by the BS Appraisal Form in front of us. This whirlwind of pessimism was purely coming from my BSF. It convinced me that every day was pointless and was going to turn out with someone else pissing me off.

I was the perfect autopilot for my BSF and so often convinced myself that something was going to be bad before it had even happened. This did so much damage to my reputation and resulted in me being left out of important meetings because my leadership peers viewed me as too emotional and they didn't want "Old Tim" in the room when they needed to think clearly and make decisions. There are no good days to be found in "Old Tim's" experiences when my BSF was in control.

"New Tim" got to the point where he decided that enough was enough and was sick of going into every meeting ready for a scrap or wanting to avoid making any sort of contribution. Armed with my Fighting Talk plus my playlists ringing positivity in my ears, I decided that I was no longer going to allow my BSF to hold me in its grasp and ruin what are supposed to be positive and productive interactions. Using my Daily Mantras means that I refuse to believe that today could be a bad day and reinforce that, whatever happens, I can choose a positive response. They mean that I arrive for all work encounters enthusiastic and resilient to the BS that my BSF and other people might spout that previously would have got me all riled up. As a leader this was huge for me as it meant I went into all interactions clear in my own mind that other people's attitudes and behaviours reflected on them and that I didn't need to let them influence me. It also meant that, rather than walking into meetings wound up or full of defeatism, I walked in with my head held high and now opened my own meetings clearly stating the purpose of the meeting and asking what people wanted to get from it. "New Tim" is able to navigate even the most boring meetings and still get something from them, and I even empowered myself to decline some meeting invites that I knew didn't need me to be there. Imagine that: using a simple daily technique that means you don't have to sit through hours and hours of Teams calls whilst doing your e-mails wishing you were somewhere else. Your Daily Mantras give you that control and positive headspace.

'Dream the shit out of the dream.'

– PAUL WELLER

What do I need to do?

This starts with some imagination and asking yourself *"What do you want to tell yourself every day?"* Take some time to write down your answers to that question. Think broadly in terms of bigger-picture positivity and think specifically for your individual days. Three good ways to create your Daily Mantras are: -

1. How do you want to think about your day ahead?

2. What do you want to remind yourself of (i.e. to remember that things are not as bad as your BSF says they are)?

3. What do you want to tell yourself that you will do today?

Then use your answers to choose your Daily Mantras and then repeat them to yourself every day. I suggest doing this as early in the day as you can as it sets you up for the day. I also know some people who prefer to use them at the end of the day as a reflective practice and to set you up for tomorrow. How you say them to yourself is up to you. You can say them out loud, which can be really powerful although it does need some quiet space: the tube isn't necessarily a safe place to tell yourself out loud that *"I will not let anyone else's BS ruin my day"*! You can write them down and read them out or even have them e-mailed to you every day or use a cool app like Daylio to automatically remind you of them. For me personally, I challenge myself to learn them off by heart and I make them part of my daily Mindfulness routine. At the right time, when I am sitting with my thoughts and feelings, I repeat in my mind the following Daily Mantras: -

➡ *"Today is a good day."*

➡ *"I am going to do a good job today."*

➡ *"All I need to do today is be my authentic self."*

➡ *"I will remember everything I need to say."* (Specific to delivering talks)

➡ *"I will engage people and they will learn a lot today."* (Specific to facilitating workshops)

➡ *"All I have to do today is listen and ask powerful questions."* (Specific to coaching)

➡ *"I am safe."*

- *"I am loved."*
- *"I am healthy."*
- *"I am happy."*
- *"Whatever happens today, I am going home to my kids, my wife and my cat."*

They are hardly Churchillian in their prose or words and they won't help me to climb Everest, but I'm not trying to inspire an entire nation or climb a mountain. I am just trying to have a good day, every day. And that is exactly what they help me to do. Like I said before, they do not 100% guarantee that you will have a good day – the world has too many nobheads in it for anyone or anything to guarantee that! What they do is fuel your power to choose a positive response. Doing these first thing in the morning means that I can shift my anticipation of what is going to happen towards being a positive one. Even if my BSF does still pop out and start to hint at something going wrong, my Daily Mantras mean I am ready to empower myself to respond with, *"I will deal with that if it happens"* or *"If that does happen, I will respond by..."*

When done consistently, your Daily Mantras become second nature to you and contribute massively to your natural thoughts and feelings becoming more positive. They give you a good start to the day, showing your BSF that you are in charge of what you think and how you feel. They also fuel your power to choose a positive response as your day progresses and things do start to happen. This technique is one that more and more of us need to practise because it is easy to kid ourselves that we don't self-talk yet we all do it through our thoughts and feelings. The more you do it deliberately, the more you are the one talking to you NOT your BSF.

Successfully shutting the BSF down

Tania is a superstar who embodies why I do what I do. We have worked together for two and a half years at the time of writing this book, running a combination of 1-2-1 coaching and Team Coaching with her Senior Management Team. Tania is an HR Director who came to me wanting to *"not be frazzled anymore"* and to set boundaries with her colleagues. This was in 2021 and Tania was coming out of the "Covid years" seeking more positive energy and with a desire to *"get rid of some rubbish in my own headspace and manage myself more effectively"*.

As we started to work together, we identified that Tania was being triggered by people and things and her BSF was taking over by making these triggers feel more intense and forcing Tania into patterns of behaviour. This would leave her frustrated from her interactions with her peers and pushed her into a *"task, task, task"* mentality as her BSF made her believe that the only way to change things was to do more and more work. Tania ended up feeling out of balance, with her work and life becoming a blur of more and more "doing" which took her away from enjoying how hard she worked by making her feel guilty if she didn't solve everyone's problems every day. As Tania grew her awareness of her challenges, she also built her motivation to change it for herself, telling me that *"I've lost sight of who I am and what I want"* and that she really wanted to be able to *"press the 'stop button' in 'the emotional moments' to respond positively and not react emotionally"*.

It was at this point that I introduced Tania to her Daily Mantras, explaining how to create them and asking her what she wanted to be able to tell herself every day. I asked Tania to spend some time reflecting on this and come back to our next session and share them with me. Tania being Tania, she didn't just come up with Daily Mantras, she took it to the next level by also including questions to ask herself every day to prompt thought and an internal dialogue to prompt her towards positive action for herself and not just trying to solve everyone else's problems. Tania also set Daily Mantras for the start of her day and the end of the day to continually learn from her experiences. Tania's Daily Mantras included: -

➡ *"I am always good enough and I am learning every day."*

➡ *"I've got your back."*

➡ *"I am important enough to turn up for me today."*

- *"I am going to do… today for my own wellbeing and headspace."*
- *"What will I role model for me today?"*
- *"What am I going to do today to make me feel at my best?"*
- *"How can I ensure that I've got enough energy left at the end of today?"*
- *"What are three things that have been good today?"*
- *"What have I done to look after myself today?"*
- *"What can I learn from today?"*

Tania relentlessly practised using her Daily Mantras and I remember her telling me *"I HAVE TO DO THIS"* as the importance of them increased, as did the positive impact they had on Tania. It transformed how she approached her days and put her firmly in control of choosing a positive response. Using her Daily Mantras turned Tania away from *"task, task, task"*, meaning that she instead told herself *"I am responsible for my joy and happiness"*. Her Daily Mantras led her to be able to tell me *"I have remembered who I am and the game has changed for me"* in recognition of how she had shut down her BSF by choosing what she wanted to hear and feel about herself.

What do you need to make your Daily Mantras?

'Make your word count for something
May your kindness show your loving
Cause you're breathing your life all into the world.'

– STONE FOUNDATION

The Cool Stuff

Now, it's time for the Cool Stuff. The difference between this and the Quick Stuff is that these techniques go deeper. They embellish the Quick Stuff that you use every day and in the moment and build up a consistent ability to shut down your BSF. These techniques are needed less frequently but they create a positive environment for you, acting as powerful things that you do to work on yourself, and they are also there as constant reminders that the ability to shut down your BSF is always in your control. The Cool Stuff also includes techniques that you can do with your team and bring other people along your positive journey to keep the BSF shut down.

For the Cool Stuff, we are going to mix it up a bit and take a different approach. We're doing that because you need to keep your BSF guessing. If we give it any sniff that each technique is written and practised in the same way, then it will start to tell you that you already know this and it doesn't work to try and avert your attention back to believing its BS. It does this because it wants you back in your comfort zone, making you think that any cool techniques are too big a risk. Filling your heart and mind with many options for shutting down your BSF keeps your BSF guessing and makes you remember that you have all the tools you need to shut it down and keep your optimism and positivity switched on.

In the Cool Stuff, we will: -

- ➡ Do an activity that will give you some credit to be motivated to keep choosing a positive response.
- ➡ Show you how to stop doing the things you don't want to do.
- ➡ Experience a real story that is enough to make anyone slip into their BSF, and learn how my team and I chose a positive response and how you can do the same to inspire you and your team.

I work on these techniques a lot with coaching clients and they enable them to develop a broader understanding of themselves and how to choose a positive response to their thoughts and feelings. As you read the Cool Stuff, pause to think about them from your own perspective and put yourself at the heart of the activities and stories to identify for yourself how you can apply them to shut down your own BSF.

'It's frightening what the mind can start to think.'

– THE LATHUMS

1. Give yourself some credit

One thing that your BSF really doesn't like is you recognising the things that you do well. It doesn't like it because the more you recognise and give yourself credit for the things you do well, the more you are motivated and able to shut down your BSF. And I don't mean the things that everyone else sees, like hitting a target, delivering a great presentation or completing a project. You have to give yourself credit for the things that no-one else sees. The things that are internal to you and only you know about them, why you do them and how they help you.

Most mornings, I go for a swim at 6am. No-one is ever going to thank me or congratulate me on getting up early and going swimming. Yet this helps me immeasurably to shut down my BSF because not only does it help me physically, it also gives me a great start to the day mentally as I

"You have to give yourself credit for the things that no-one else sees" can work through things in my head whilst I'm under water (no distractions down there!). In fact, it fires all the positive emotions and chemicals through my heart and mind.

I also meditate for ten minutes every morning. That precious quiet time of mindfulness is something that has changed my life and is a huge strength for me in shutting down my BSF. Especially when it comes to getting my mental health back on track. Yet no client of mine is ever going to welcome me by saying *"I really appreciate you doing that mindfulness this morning, Tim, to put you in the headspace and be confident about doing a really good job for us today."*

So often when I am in coaching conversations or facilitating a team session, I am listening but my head is filled with all sorts of thoughts and is trying to distract me. I always allow those thoughts to pass me by and don't get distracted, staying focused on listening and being ready to respond with a question or some feedback or suggestions that relate to what the other person/people have just said. A big part of my job is being able to impact people by how I respond to what they tell me about themselves or the challenges they face. Yet none of my LinkedIn recommendations say, *"Tim always allows his thoughts to pass by and he never gets distracted when we're having a conversation. He always focuses on me"*. It is up to me to recognise the strength for listening to people that I have and show my BSF that, as much as it might try to steal my attention, I will recognise myself for choosing to stay focused on other people and keep building that strength so my BSF knows it can't win.

Before I go into a 1-2-1 coaching conversation or I am about to facilitate a workshop or just before going on stage to deliver a talk or host a conference, I will be nervous as hell. To quote an ex-colleague of mine, I am sometimes *"shaking like a shitting dog"*. To overcome those nerves, I find a quiet space for a few minutes, often in the gents' toilet and take a breath. I use my Daily Mantras to ground myself and get rid of my nerves before I do the work that people have booked me to do. Whilst I will get recognised for delivering a good coaching session or for engaging an audience, they will never say, *"Thanks for going to the toilet for a few minutes before we started and getting rid of your nerves"*. Only I know that I do that and only I can give myself credit for doing so to motivate me to keep going.

The more you give yourself a pat on the back for the things that no-one else sees, the more your confidence grows. We all want feedback from others, but it always starts with you and you are the only person who battles your BSF so you have to choose to give yourself the proverbial pat on the back for the things you do well. This isn't about creating an ego or being arrogant, this is about having positive dialogue with yourself and seeing the positive things that you do that no-one else sees.

Give yourself some credit activity

What are the things that you do that no-one else sees that you need to give yourself some credit for? Write them down, create a habit for recognising yourself consistently. Consider here the things that you do that help you to be at your best and have a good impact on others. And the things that you do that help others without them knowing. Choose how often to do this and set reminders to stop and give yourself some credit. Don't wait for others to do it – do it for yourself to keep that BSF quiet.

What do you need to give yourself some credit for?

'Get up and get involved
It's now or never
It's time to make that change
Get in this together.'

– PAUL WELLER

2. Create your Stop Doing List

We all love a list. Whether it is a shopping list or a list of things to pack for our holidays, we write lists and lists and believe that just by writing them, we will transform ourselves into ultra-organised people who get shit done. The classic to-do list is a favourite of mine. For many people, their days at work start by writing a to-do list for all the things that they will get done today. Or a list of things that *"I have to get done today"*. When you then get to the end of the day and have done very few or none of the things on the to-do list, it leaves you feeling frustrated and like you have not done anything that day. At that point, you write another to-do list for the day after and repeat and repeat until your days are consumed by lists of all of the things that you're not getting done. My BSF used to love a to-do list. I would sit and write them out every day and gladly tick them off on the occasions that I managed to get a few things done on my list. It even told me that I was dead smart because I learnt to use Tasks in Microsoft Outlook, so now instead of writing out lists, I had electronic reminders that would pop up at allocated times to remind me of what I still hadn't done.

The problem with to-do lists is your BSF will infiltrate your thoughts and feelings and make you look at them differently. They are supposed to focus you and give you a sense of achievement as you work through them. The reality is that your BSF makes you see them as *"I've got loads to do"* and makes you precious about them as if the only thing that matters is your to-do list. Your BSF takes your to-do lists and turns them into pressure that you put on yourself. The reminders that you set for yourself to tick off your to-do list cut like a knife as you realise that it is still just as long as it was that morning and maybe even getting longer.

I used to work with a manager who had an entire book full of her to-do lists and, every morning and every night, she would sit and update them, which basically meant she was repeating the same meaningless task at least twice a day. She would carry this book around with her and use it to make notes in her meetings, so it was then full of actions from meetings to do on top of all her other tasks. It was like her ball and chain that she took everywhere with her. I'd love to tell you that this particular colleague was effective and her to-do lists separated her from her peers, getting more done and engaging with people in a positive way. Was she bollocks! She was one of the worst people I have ever worked with. Stressed to the max every day and dull in how she communicated; she could never even answer a question without flicking through her book of lists as if that would solve everything. Unfortunately, all it did tell her was what she still hadn't done yet.

Like anything, when shutting down your BSF, you have to choose the lists to write that will actually help you. Your BSF wants you to write more and more lists of the things that you are yet to do because that breaks your motivation and is a sneaky way of your BSF "keeping you in your lane" and not taking any risks. Most people who write lists expect them to trigger some sort of inspiration in them but usually end up giving up because they start to believe that positive change and achieving things is beyond them. Their BSF keeps them in their risk-free comfort zone by blinding them with more and more lists of the things they will need to do to make that positive change. If I wrote a list of all of the things that I have had to do to write two books and do a job that I love, I would still be writing it when I died!!

The BS of the world has convinced us that we need lists and your BSF takes that and twists it in your mind. We get a dopamine hit from ticking something off a list, so we chase that instant gratification by making more lists. Tech companies have found a way to sell us more lists as productivity tools are rammed down our throats, making promises to make our lives easier when in fact your Trello boards and Monday dashboards are just more and more lists.

We even wear lists on our wrists these days as our smart watches tell us to check our heart rate and how many steps we have taken. So many people lose so much time trying to tick off so many lists that their days are a vicious circle of feeling like they get nothing done, which then powers up the BSF production line. Our BSF convinces us to kid ourselves that to-do lists will give us joy when, in reality, they become a stick to beat ourselves up with as they just remind us of what we've still not done.

'Your choices aren't full of time, time is full of your choices.'

– PAUL PHELAN

The most important list you can write to shut down your BSF is your Stop Doing List. This is a list of all of the things that you will stop doing to give you more confidence and take control back from your BSF. When I have done this for myself and with coaching clients, examples of items that go on the Stop Doing List include: -

- Stop catastrophising
- Stop replying to e-mails like my life depends on it
- Stop interrupting people
- Stop doing all the talking at meetings
- Stop chasing my team for things before I need them
- Stop answering my boss's calls after 6pm
- Stop believing my negative thoughts and feelings
- Stop writing to-do lists

Your Stop Doing List can be so liberating for you as it frees you from the mundanity and repetitive BS that comes from your BSF. It also releases you from the barriers that you are putting up for yourself and shows you the things you can stop doing to give you the freedom in your own heart and mind to start doing the things that make a positive difference to you whilst telling your to-do list loving BSF to fuck right off.

Create your Stop Doing List Activity

Write down all of the things that you want to stop doing. Ask yourself, "What are the things that I can stop doing today that will make tomorrow better for me?" Think about the things that are holding you back. The things that cause you stress and frustration. You can even go practical with this and look at your calendar for the last month and pick out the pinch points of meetings and interactions that cause you some consternation. Once you have done that, choose what you can stop doing to make those experiences what you want them to be. Look at your life outside of work and choose the things that you can stop doing to help you to respond to your negative thoughts and feelings. The key with your Stop Doing List is only putting things on there that YOU will stop doing. This isn't a wishlist for what you want other people to stop doing, it is YOUR Stop Doing List.

That's what makes it so powerful. Perhaps you have a colleague who you would like to stop ranting at meetings.

Well, you can't make them stop; what you can do is stop reacting to it. Stop getting involved. Maybe it is that you should stop avoiding giving them feedback on how their rants ruin the meetings for you and everyone else. You can't stop other people being negative in the office, but you can stop yourself from being negative and stop yourself from taking part in those negative conversations.

There is always something that you can choose to stop doing that releases you from the grip of your BSF. Take some time today to write your Stop Doing List and see how it empowers you to be who you really want to be. This can also be a fun thing to do with your team so create a shared Stop Doing List of all the things that will make work better for you as a team.

What needs to be on your Stop Doing List?

'Don't stop thinking about tomorrow
Don't stop, it'll soon be here
It'll be better than before
Yesterday's gone, yesterday's gone.'

– FLEETWOOD MAC

3. Build your Wall of Inspiration

Let's now really hammer your BSF by showing you how to do something that it particularly hates – having fun and finding inspiration when all around you are losing their heads and the situation seems to be going from bad to worse.

Picture the scene, it's one many people can relate to, you are part of a team that is growing. Through your own success, the team is getting bigger and bigger with more people joining and more responsibility being given to us. As part of the leadership group for this team, I was involved in conversations about us running out of space and soon not having enough desks for people to work from in the office. This was before hybrid working became a thing and the boss I worked for at the time (Incompetent Ian – remember him from *volume 1*?!) was not one for trusting people to work from home!

So, we had to find a solution. Many were put forward. Reasonable requests for us to move into bigger, local locations that the company owned and were not being fully used all fell on deaf ears. As did the suggestion for people who were travelling from far and wide to work at the current office to be based at other company locations more local to them, freeing up some desk space. We're going proper "back in the day" here when everyone was expected to be in the office every day (those were the days, eh?!) and, typical of the wheeler-dealer type that Incompetent Ian was, rather than come up with a solution that actually worked, he returned from a work trip to Dublin to tell us how he had found his own solution. He had procured a Portakabin for free that was going to be transported and put in the warehouse where up to six people could work.

As Ian beamed with pride telling everyone how he had solved all of our problems, everyone realised that someone was going to have to actually work in this Portakabin once it arrived. This caused a lot of speculation about the state of the Portakabin and who was most likely to move into it. It also made people try to get their case in early, justifying why they shouldn't be the ones to move into there, including some quite vehement arguments at the managers' meeting. There was BS galore coming from the collective BSF as people either complained about something that hadn't happened yet or sulked expecting to be the ones who were to be moved into the Portakabin. Ian kept his cards close to his chest and just sat there with a smug grin on his face refusing to share who would be the *"lucky team who will get their own office"*. I refused to get caught up in it all as, by that point, I was Breaking the Mould and I knew Ian well enough to fully expect that it would be my team and me who would be relocated. I did my best to pacify my team as the speculation and BS grew, choosing to focus instead on doing a good job. I decided to worry about our impending move into a Portakabin when it was confirmed that it was actually happening.

To put this into context, this wasn't a fancy new Portakabin that was being provided for us and nor was it going to have its own place outside the office (you know, like where most Portakabins are). Oh no – this Portakabin was over 20 years old, had sat unused in a car park in Dublin for the last five years and it was going to be housed inside a noisy warehouse. You see, where we were based at this time was at a training academy in a repurposed old warehouse building. In Widnes. A warehouse that was freezing cold as it had no heating and a massive door that was open all day. HGV trucks came in and out to be repainted, which also gave it a lovely whiff of paint and burning plastic most days.

'As you dream your dream tonight
Let tomorrow look me right in the eye.'

– PAOLO NUTINI

The Portakabin arrived and our worst fears were confirmed. Its arrival was announced and we all went into the warehouse to see it being delivered and placed into its new position at the back of the warehouse. What we had been told about the Portakabin didn't do it justice – it was a proper shithole. The windows were either missing, broken or covered in some sort of dark mess that can only be described as "shit". It had no door on it and the carpet looked like a combination of vomit stains and bird shit. I genuinely can't paint a bad enough picture of this Portakabin and, to top it all off, it absolutely stank. And I mean it reeked... of a combination of B.O. and piss. We all looked at each other, sighing and laughing with incredulity as we anticipated who was being given this as their new home.

The following day, my worst fears were confirmed. Ian came bounding into the office and in front of my team and everyone else in earshot announced, *"Tim, you and your team are going into the Portakabin because the Driver Training and Recruitment team are more important and I need them around me"*. He finished off with some sort of attempted sarcasm and encouraged everyone to take the piss out of us before walking off. Yes, he did genuinely deliver the news to us by telling us that we were less important than other people. Ian really was a walking, talking BSF.

'Don't fall into the trap of thinking you need to wear a "happy mask" all the time.'

– BETH LANG

I accepted it and got my team together to rally us, encouraging us all to see it as a *"fuck you"* moment; let's use it to show how important we are. We could demonstrate how resilient and mature we were as a team as we all agreed not to moan about it to anyone else or bite on the bait when people started talking to us about it or taking the piss. We also called out the reality of the situation, which was that it was going to be weeks before the Portakabin was in any way ready for people to work in it, so why be bothered by something that is weeks away from becoming reality?

As one of my team, the wonderful Nik Donoghue, remarked, *"We'll be fine, Tim. We'll make it better than anyone else's office and it keeps us away from the distractions of being in here with everyone else"*. Nik was always someone who inspired me and would see the light in the darkness, helping us all to shut down our BSF. If you ever get to work with a Nik; do everything you can to learn as much as you can from them.

To give Ian some credit, he kept his promise to get the Portakabin painted and the windows and carpet replaced. It did indeed take weeks for us to actually move in because, whilst Ian got the aesthetics sorted, he forgot that we needed electricity and broadband to be connected to the "new" Portakabin. Of course, Ian delegated this to me and I spent weeks of frustrating ticket raising and phone calls with IT trying to convince them that *"Yes, we are moving into a Portakabin that is inside a warehouse, 200 metres away from the closest network point and has no electricity"*. You can probably imagine what my BSF was doing to me alongside my busy day job. I now had to project manage an IT and electrical installation into a stinking Portakabin inside a freezing cold warehouse!

We were finally ready to go and our desks and everything else were moved in for us over a weekend so a Monday morning could be our first day working in our new office. It was functional enough and we made it home with a mini fridge and tea pot. We got on with our jobs as best we could in the face of constant piss-taking from our colleagues. Ian had started ringing me every five minutes to ask me questions that he already knew the answer to but could no longer walk over to my desk and have one conversation with me to sort them out.

Here is what it was like to work in that bloody Portakabin:

- It was freezing cold. We were moved in there in winter and our portable heaters either did nothing because the Portakabin had no door on it or the fumes coming from them made it unbearable to have them on for more than ten minutes. So we all sat there working in our coats and gloves!
- We were constantly interrupted by truck drivers arriving at the warehouse and not knowing where to go. They were always told by the team painting the trucks to go and see us in the Portakabin even though we had nothing to do with them and they needed to go to another office which was based over the road. Adding to the confusion, a lot of these drivers couldn't speak English!
- It had no printer so every time we needed to print something we had to walk 100 metres and up two flights of stairs. We would often then find that someone was in the middle of a big print job. This was a real problem for us as my team was responsible for a lot of operational training that regularly needed training records printed so the training could be done to the right safety standards.
- It still stank of B.O. and piss. OK, the smell was weaker than when the Portakabin first arrived, but it was like it was stained into the walls and you could not get rid of it. Add to that, the fact that we

were based in Widnes. No disrespect to the town of Widnes but it stinks. It is well known for it due to the chemical factories in the town. Not only that, but we also had a glue factory on the same industrial unit that let out the most awful smell you can imagine which then seeped in through the open warehouse doors.

'Raise your mind to free your soul.'

– BOBBY HARDEN AND THE SOULFUL SAINTS

Just stop and imagine what working in that god-awful Portakabin would do to you and your team. Then consider what my BSF was doing to me as I set off for another day at work full of constant interruptions, those smells and the additional time it put onto us just doing our jobs. On one particular day, when the smells and frustrations were getting the better of us, we stopped and spoke about our situation and how much it was getting in the way of doing our jobs but also how we didn't want to let it get us down. Between us we came up with the idea of using some of the space in the Portakabin to inspire us and turn the shithole into somewhere that reminded us of the good things in our lives that we could use to be more positive and optimistic every day.

That's when we came up with the Wall of Inspiration. For us, this was part of our whiteboard wall that we had and, alongside the lists of our training courses and performance targets, we installed a collection of: -

- Pictures of our family
- Pictures of people and things that inspire us
- Inspirational quotes
- Song lyrics that mean something to us
- Covers of our favourite books
- Pictures of our favourite places

This transformed the smelly shithole into somewhere that made us believe we could do a really good job and enjoy what we did, even in such difficult circumstances. Now the Portakabin included a combination of all the things that meant something to us personally. We each took turns placing our chosen items on the Wall of Inspiration and telling each other what they meant to us. This meant that my team and I talked about our grandparents and children. We also shared more about our cultural influences and why they inspired us. It also gave us the chance to laugh a little at each other's favourite music or places. It gave us something to keep adding to, to get to know each other more and to share in each other's inspiration.

That is exactly what a Wall of Inspiration does for you. It gives you that urge to do something positive, even when you're up against it and working in an environment that feeds your BSF, you can still choose to be inspired and still choose to make that environment something that means something to you.

You can build your Wall of Inspiration with your team or for yourself. I have many coaching clients who have created their Wall of Inspiration on the wall behind their laptop screens at home so, when they are working in isolation, they can look up and see those people and things that mean much more to them than what is going on during their latest Teams call. It really helps you to stay self-motivated when the BSF brings in the dark days. It is a great visual way of reminding yourself that, in a world that can become tainted by your BSF, you still have a great number of things that inspire you and create positive emotions for you.

Build your Wall of Inspiration Activity

Build your Wall of Inspiration today using a whiteboard, a pinboard, a blank wall, a flipchart or even do it digitally and have it as your screensaver. Choosing all of the people and things that you know creates an urge in you to do something positive. If you are ever on a virtual workshop or a call with me, you will see some of my Wall of Inspiration behind me so I can see it on screen whilst I work remotely. I also have other walls that only I can see in my home office that are covered with images that mean I am surrounded by inspiration. Some teams have done this remotely and they each take turns to share their screens to show a PowerPoint slide with their inspiration on and talk their teammates through it. When you do this together, you can help to bring it to life for each other.

What and who will be on your Wall of Inspiration?

'I've waited, and given the chance again,
I'd do it all the same, but either way
I'm always outplayed, up on your down days,
I left it the right way, to start again.'

– EMBRACE

What have we done in this chapter

- Shown how you have to choose your mindset to shut down your BSF
- Ditched the judgement of ourselves to power how we respond to our BSF
- Tried out some activities that get you started on shutting down your BSF
- Worked on the Quick Stuff that you can start doing today
- Introduced you to the Cool Stuff that will really make the difference to you

Coaching questions to get you thinking about shutting down your BSF

- When do you most need to shut down your BSF?
- How will you positively respond to avoid the battle of resisting your BSF?
- Where can you put the Quick Stuff into practice for you?
- What will the Cool Stuff do for you in terms of shutting down your BSF?

- ➡ How much better will your life and confidence be when you shut down your BSF by using the techniques in this chapter?

CHAPTER FIVE

WHEN THE BULLSHIT FACTORY TAKES HOLD OF LEADERS AND TEAMS AND HOW TO SHUT IT DOWN

'So, take my hand now, understand now
You can come here too
C'mon people we're making it now
If only you could be with us.'

– RICHARD ASHCROFT (FT. LIAM GALLAGHER)

Now we turn our attention to the profound impact that the BSF has on businesses. In this chapter, I'm going to take you on a BSF safari and show you how BSF operates in the wild, in one of its favourite habitats: Leaders and Teams. This is where I see it most prevalent in the work that I do. So many of the problems in organisations can be traced back to how the collective BSF effect turns leaders and teams into the kind of people that they never intended to be.

Now you know how to shut down your personal BSF, I want to leave you with demonstrations of how it infiltrates where people spend most of their time. I will share examples of how I help leaders and teams to shut it down so their collective experience is much closer to the one they actually want when they go to work.

This chapter shines the light on how the BSF infiltrates leaders and teams. When many BSFs come together it can create an explosion of negativity. Especially when they are led by a leader whose BSF production line is functioning. I will show you some classic examples of a BSF in action in leaders and teams that will make you think, and you will no doubt relate to. To close the chapter, I will share with you the five pillars of leadership that are the foundation for the work I do and demonstrate how they can shut down the BSF so you can lead how you want to lead and work in a team that you want to be part of.

'It's better people, love one another
'Cause livin' your life can be tough
It's better people, speak to each other.'

– OASIS

Being a leader is a true privilege. When you are a leader, you get to directly impact how people feel at work, how they perform and what they achieve in their career. What a privilege to be given that opportunity and the responsibility to make those things a positive experience. The leaders you work with have a huge influence on how you think and feel, yet some can directly contribute to switching on your BSF, especially if their BSF is in operation.

Working in a team is meant to be good. It is a group of people choosing to spend their time together with the aim of achieving the same goals or helping the same people. The old adage of spending more time at work than with your family is true for the vast majority of us and that means that you spend most of your time with your teammates. Even if it is now predominantly through the MS Teams rectangle, your teammates make a big impression on how you experience your work.

I feel so much empathy for people who go to work and end up being the leader they don't want to be or who are part of a team where it feels more of a battle than a pleasure. A lot of my empathy here comes from having been that leader and having worked in many teams just like that! This is where my passion really comes to life, and I want this book to help leaders and teams to shut down their individual and collective BSF to empower themselves to be the leaders and teams that they want to be.

It is actually a lot easier than it sounds because it is achieved through the positive choices we can make no matter where we work. I will show you how real leaders and teams have shut down their BSF. First, we have to call out the utter BS that exists in leaders and teams. We'll do this by looking at classic examples that I am sure you will be able to relate to. Then we'll dig into five key areas where leaders and teams can choose a positive response to their BSF production line to make work feel like they want it to feel. I'll share some true stories of leaders and teams that I have worked with to get you thinking about how shutting down your BSF can help you in the work that you do.

"Leadership and teams can end up full of BS because they are full of people"

'No-one is good at everything. Everyone is good at something.'

– NOEL GALLAGHER

Classic BSF in Leaders and Teams

Leadership and teams can end up full of BS because they are full of people. And all people bring one thing to work – their own BSF and their human trigger points. These get set off by spending more time with more people whose BSF is playing up. It can often start with a leader who is operating from their own BSF which then permeates out across the rest of the team. It can also emanate from team members. We have all worked with the kind of team that are full of the *"that's how we do things around here"* brigade and take pride in refusing to accept any new leaders into their team.

Have a quick game of BS bingo by "dabbing" (or "dobbing" depending on your preference) off the things below that you have seen in leaders and teams: -

- Working in silos
- Criticising their own teams and doing nothing to change it

- Moaning about the things that are within their control
- Not calling out negative attitudes and behaviours
- Never giving constructive feedback or positive recognition
- Doing their e-mails on Teams calls and in meetings
- Trying to do everything themselves and not delegating
- Micromanaging people
- Only ever talking about tasks
- Cancelling 1-2-1's

The list could go on! All of the above can be traced back to the BSF. If you asked leaders and teams if they wanted to be known for doing any of those things, you would be very hard-pushed to find someone who said *"yes"*. Yet all around the world, those things are happening. Right now, today. Whilst you're reading this book, someone's BSF is making leaders and teams be known for the things that they don't want to be known for.

'Yeah, I've been working all week,
I'm shot
Yeah, I've been working all week,
for what?'

– HARD-FI

The impact of the BSF pervades company cultures as leaders and teams become blind to what products their negative thoughts and feelings are leading them to. You can play your own game of BSF Bingo with the things that leaders and teams say. Here are some classic BSF examples that you might be able to spot where you have worked:

- *"I can't change, that's just me."* – This is usually said in defence of their behaviour or resistance to change.
- Leaders who say *"there is nothing I can do, my team are just like that."* – The beauty of the BSF reveals itself as the fear of having an honest conversation becomes the reason (or rather the excuse) for not being able to work on their team to change their performance and behaviours.

- *"That's just the way it is here,"* or *"that's just how 'they' are."* – These are Grade A excuses for the wrong attitudes and behaviours being accepted in an organisation.
- *"I'll do your appraisal when you do something wrong."* – This basically tells you not to expect any recognition for anything good whilst also admitting that they don't feel comfortable giving feedback.
- *"I've been to loads of these training courses before."* – This is a great way of blaming others for the fact that you can't be arsed to do anything different and your BSF keeps you repeating the behaviours that you know don't really work.
- People who are always talking about how *"senior leaders should do this and my boss should do that,"* only to then never do those things themselves!

Two more personal favourites of mine are when you come back from a week's holiday and it's like people have been waiting for you to come back instead of doing something for themselves. They approach you with the obligatory *"Did you have a good holiday?"* and, before you can even answer, they follow it up with *"Did you see my e-mail?"* Sigh. *"No, because I was on holiday, you dickhead,"* is how you want to respond but instead you allow their BSF driving their lack of accountability to kick yours into action as you feel a sense of guilt for not reading their e-mail whilst on holiday or prioritising it over the other 300 e-mails that you've had since you were last in work!

Why do you think so many people at work adopt a "cover-my-arse" mentality and are constantly trying to prove themselves to the boss? It is because their BSF makes them think and feel that what they are doing is not good enough so you must prove to someone else that it is. This leads to them telling their boss about everything they have done, which then triggers the boss's BSF into thinking that either they can't be trusted to do anything without being told or that they have a lack of confidence, meaning they start to think that they are not good enough either.

How many of these BSF-driven attitudes and behaviours have you seen in your leaders and teams?

- CC'ing senior leaders into their e-mails (not sure what's worse – this or when people click "Reply All" even though they only need to tell one person!)
- Never picking up the phone to actually talk to people in an impromptu conversation because they want everything written down or on a Teams Call / meeting agenda
- Only looking at things from their own point of view
- Being overly competitive with people who are ultimately on the same side

- Telling you *"to be careful of"* others. "Others" to whom they won't say to their face what they say behind their backs!
- Deliberately not doing something because you don't like someone

This BS floats around leaders and teams like air and can easily influence others to follow the BSF examples in front of them. There is no way that if you asked people how they want to behave at work, they would say any of the above. However, people end up doing all of that because the dynamics of working with different people fire up the emotions that their BSF feeds off and grasps the opportunity to take over with both hands.

'It's all bullshit but we all still pretend.'

– GERRY CINNAMON

Allow me to introduce you to some real BSF-induced examples of leaders and teams:

One rule for me, one rule for you

The work Christmas party – always a virile breeding ground for the BSF. I saw first-hand when I was working for an organisation that employed around 250 people all based in the fancy HQ (the building where people work that used to be called an "office"!). The demographic of the workforce was one of the younger generations. The CEO's mantra of *"party hard, work hard"* was embraced by the majority of the people who worked there. Free drinks were often the order of the day. Nothing wrong with that, and I was always the first at the bar in my younger days, but I have often had to live through the damage that a pissed-up BSF can do to leaders and teams. By this stage in my career and my life, my RSVP to the Christmas do was always a "no thanks."

This organisation was full of contradictions in its culture and the *"party hard, work hard"* mantra was in itself an oxymoron for the all-controlling CEO as, from what I saw, he couldn't even handle his ale and he expected his C-Suite and Senior Leaders to be available 24-hours a day. He was a leader whose BSF embodied the *"what I say goes but what I do doesn't matter"* approach as his behaviour was often at odds with what he asked of his employees and said publicly about himself and the brand.

'One man's truth
Is another man's waste of time.'

– GERRY CINNAMON

So, the work Christmas party is arranged and becomes the talk of the office as the Saturday night date approaches. The week leading up to the party sees the CEO bring his C-Suite together at the office for their last board meeting of the year and, fair play to them, they make sure they spend time recognising people and communicating with everyone about the year's performance and initial plans for the year ahead. This lifts the mood for everyone at what is a very busy time of year and, whether you are going to the party or not, you feel part of something and appreciate the comms from the execs.

That evening, the C-Suite were being taken out for a meal by the CEO to spend some social time together. Also, fair play to them as senior leaders need to build strong bonds and get to know each other out of work. I tell my exec to have a good night and head off home for the day.

That "fair play" sentiment soon turns to "for fuck's sake" the following morning as the talk around the office is all about the C-Suite night out, which has been played out on social media. Highlights include them being plied with copious amounts of alcohol by the CEO and one of them falling asleep at a table in a restaurant. The final coverage is of them in a strip-bar where the CEO is literally throwing money about.

I personally have no problem with people getting drunk and going to a strip-bar (we've all been there!). What you do in your time is up to you and no-one got hurt and, despite the brazenness of it all, it appears nothing was inappropriate. But why on earth would you choose to plaster it all over social media? It was shared via the CEO's own channels where he had hundreds of thousands of followers, including employees and customers. I'll tell you why – because his BSF told him it was a good idea. A good idea to show off getting people wasted and doing risqué things. Again, that's fine in your own time with your own mates, but when you are the exec leaders of a multi-million-pound business who bleat on about how people need to behave and come down hard on people making mistakes, then you have walked straight into your BSF's devious plan to make you look like a right dickhead. And it worked, as the atmosphere in work the following day was one of nervousness and disappointment as most people spent the day trying to keep their head down, pretending they hadn't seen last night's antics on Instagram whilst the dickheads who were there celebrated it like it was something to be proud of.

What compounded it for me that day was that we were finishing a development programme with some of the organisation's leading talent who were completing a six-month programme and their Exec had been invited to attend the final day and give feedback to them. Unfortunately for him, he was the one who had fallen under the CEO's spell the night before and when we finally got someone to find out where he was, we were simply told, *"He's asleep in his hotel. Didn't get in until 6am and isn't coming in today"*. I appreciate the honesty but maybe try to sugarcoat it a little when telling a group of people that he couldn't be arsed to recognise their hard work because he's too weak to know when he's had enough.

If you think that is bad enough, then this BSF shit isn't over yet. The Christmas party took place the following weekend and guess what happened? Yes, thanks to the "role model behaviour" of the C-Suite and the free bar, some people took it a bit too far, resulting in the venue staff being spat at and some fights happening. Two people got caught shagging in the toilet and two others were kicked out for sniffing cocaine off the bar. Sounds like a good night, right? Not when it's with people you work with and you have to return to face them on Monday morning! The venue itself took its revenge by posting their disgust on social media, including pictures of the damage done and telling the world that this particular well-known brand was not welcome back at their establishment.

That Monday morning was a mix of gossip and crisis meetings. And this is where the BSF really shows itself in its true light. The CEO was at the centre of the crisis meeting demanding that HR take disciplinary action against those who took it too far. Yes, the CEO who spent last week telling people via his own behaviour that it was OK to act like a drunken tosser, not caring what example that sets to the other people who you work with, was now chief disciplinarian and expected some people to be fired as a result of what had happened at the party that he paid for. He had even shown off about how much he'd spent on booze for everyone!

Here is the best bit, clearly illustrating how a BSF takes over leaders and teams in this whole situation. HR went ahead and tried to take disciplinary action against those identified as doing the worst things at the Christmas party. That is hard at the best of times as employment law doesn't tend to cover *"pissed up behaviour due to free booze provided by my employer"* and everyone had a defence of *"they started it"* and could point to the C-Suite to suggest that they were only doing what had been role modelled to them a few nights earlier. HR could have chosen to give the CEO some much-needed feedback and suggested an open, mature comms would have helped everyone to move on. But no, their own BSF kicked in through fear and submission and they spent months wasting time on awkward, fruitless disciplinary meetings which killed the atmosphere for many teams and made it impossible for leaders to hold people to account and ultimately resulted in more good people leaving the organisation.

Those bar bills in December were probably peanuts compared to how much it cost in time and lost productivity. Not to mention the cost incurred trying to replace the good people who left as a result.

'As each day goes by
A little more
You can't remember
What it was you wanted, anyway.'

– THE JAM

The competition for who can have the shittest day at work

This is a game played all over the world as the global influence of the BSF makes us think we have to be the winner for who has the worst day or who is the busiest. I have lost track of the number of times I have asked a simple introductory question to start a conversation with a leader, such as *"how are you?"*, only to be bombarded with responses like *"I'm really busy"* or *"I've got a lot on"* and the tried and tested *"there's not enough hours in the day"*. It's like *"Christ, all I did was ask how you are, not what you're doing with your time!!!"* and people become completely oblivious to this and use it as the slogan they become known for. It's like there is a "cult of the busy" that people have joined!

Now, people are busy and leaders and teams will have a lot on, that is reality. No-one goes to work to sit on their arse doing sweet FA all day (let me guess – your BSF has just told you that some people do go to work to do sweet FA?!! They don't. It's just that other people's BSF allows them to come across that way because no-one holds them accountable for not doing anything). What your BSF does is make you intensify that sense of being busy and use it as a badge of honour to show how important you are and / or defend you from someone else asking you to do something else.

Most people use the "busyness" lines because they hear other people say it all the time. The leader who tells everyone how busy they are leads a team who tells everyone how busy they are. I see this often in Team Coaching sessions when the "busyness" rears its head amongst peers and a BSF tidal wave goes around the room as everyone strives to get a one-up on their peers for how busy they are and how bad they have it. This is just your BSF playing ping-pong with everyone else's BSF. It doesn't want you to break the mould and take the risk of being perceived as the only one who isn't busy. Or stand out from your "busyness" comfort zone by being the one who holds their peers to account by asking them "what can we do about it?" to lead to a positive challenge rather than your BSF making you just agree with everyone else and submit your own entry to the "shittest day at work" competition.

'Caught up in this life
Years we get busy.'

– STEREOPHONICS

This is your BSF-loving life as it takes over your thoughts and feelings and produces those reactive attitudes and behaviours. It doesn't stop there though as the "busy fools" that leaders and teams become only blinds them to what happens as a result of their "busyness" contest. Telling everyone how busy you are all the time makes you less approachable to others and people start their conversations with you with things like *"Sorry, I know you're really busy"* and start sending you more emails and inviting you to more Teams calls instead of talking to you and dealing with things quickly. Of course, they won't just get on and do things because the angst of the leader's "busyness" makes other people afraid of trying something in case that angst gets taken out on them. This really is a vicious circle being stirred by everyone's BSF.

To top this all off, the BSF then also starts to interview people who want to join the organisation. The leaders and teams who are the "busyness" champions sit in interviews with potential new team members and lie their arses off about how wonderful it is to work there. The *"we're all too busy"* becomes *"it's a great place to work with lots of opportunities"* as their BSF tells them that the new recruit is their saviour and will soon be as busy as them so you must manipulate them into thinking this is the best place for them to work. Fast forward six months and said new recruits are now mid-table in the "busyness" league and wondering where the "great place to work" has gone.

I wonder how much money an organisation could save and how much productivity they could get back if, instead of wasting time telling everyone how busy they were, those leaders and teams spent time on actually doing what they are there to do – work together in a way that leads to results and engagement.

'Never let a clock tell you
what you got time for
It only goes around, goes around,
goes around.'

– FONTAINES D.C.

When BSF gets you to fake it

Don't roll out the red carpet for the execs

"We've got important visitors coming in tomorrow. Please make sure there are no coats on the back of chairs, no-one eats at their desks and there are no bins overflowing," read the regular e-mail we would all get at a particular organisation when customers were being brought in for a whistle-stop tour of the head office. At the time, my team and I were based right outside the CEO's office and would get it sent to us like everyone else and then we'd receive a follow-up in person from the dragon that was the CEO's PA. Then we would get another e-mail from my boss's boss just to make sure we got the message that some visitors were coming in.

This is the classic BSF approach of "don't let them see what it's really like!" We never got thanked for doing as we were told and no-one recognised how we decided to stop this BS and just asked our teams to live up to these standards every day instead of scrambling around like idiots just because someone who had no idea who we were was chaperoned into the CEO's office without even looking at us. This specific example goes on across lots of organisations and shows the lengths that your BSF will go to to cover up something that either doesn't actually matter or that your CEO and customers need to see so they can help you to make it better.

Don't show the execs what's really happening

I remember reading a story about how a previous Chairman of Sainsbury's would visit their supermarkets and would be met with spotless floors, aisles clear of people replacing products and even tins and boxes all facing the same way on the shelves. The Chairman recognised this as BS because he had worked in retail for more than 50 years. To combat this, he began visiting their stores incognito so he could see the problems their staff and customers faced for real so he could lead on helping them to make it better.

Your BSF wants you to cover up the problems because it creates that doom-ridden anticipation of a bollocking, yet the people whose help you need to solve the problems can only help you if they can see the problems for themselves. Your BSF tells you that the Chairman wants to see everything is perfect only for you to then let it go back to rack and ruin once they have left, allowing you to moan that the Chairman hadn't sorted it out for you! Your BSF makes you forget that the biggest bollockings you are scared of are the ones that you never actually get.

Your BSF is wonderful at tricking you into thinking that Senior Leaders or customers in your organisations are some sort of celestial being and you place them on a pedestal forgetting that they are, in fact, human just like you. You become afraid of speaking to them and sharing what you really think because your BSF makes them appear like the parent or Head Teacher who had so much authority over

“Your BSF makes you forget that the biggest bollockings you are scared of are the ones that you never actually get” you in your formative years. I love it when organisations waste loads of money on anonymous feedback surveys and nothing ever gets done about the results because no-one knows who said what and no-one has the courage to tell the senior leaders what is preventing the culture from being what it could be.

This is a classic example of your BSF pulling the blindfold over your eyes and making you forget that an organisation is just a place where people choose to go and be paid for their efforts. It doesn't dictate your life to you or get to decide your attitudes for you and how you behave. Yet your BSF tells you to allow it to do exactly that to you. And then you moan about it at the same time!

Oh, how people love to take it personally when an organisation treats them badly. I know I did for many years and would allow what happened at work to completely take over my life and worship at the altar of the dickheads who I was afraid of saying anything to. I spent years just covering my arse as I anticipated the senior leaders (most of whom didn't even know my name and still won't!) where I worked had this God-like presence and authority over me. A great sign of a BSF in action in your organisation is when people use senior leaders' names to get things done. I have had the names of William, Dave, Rob and lots more put into the sentence *"X wants it done"* as a way of motivating me to drop everything and get something that isn't important to what I do completed as a matter of urgency.

Don't challenge the execs

One of the moments when I realised I had to start shutting down my BSF in this area was when I was told that I no longer needed to spend time every week producing a report and sending it out to over 50 Area Managers. The reason given for this was, and I quote, *"X left last week and there was only her that wanted the report. No-one else does anything with it. Not sure she even did. Now she's left, it doesn't matter anymore"*. My incredulous response to this was, *"Did no-one think to question this before? I have been sending that report out every week for three fucking years"*. I just got a shrug of shoulders as a response and was basically told to do whatever someone with perceived authority asked for next.

Organisations spend so much time looking for cost savings and to increase their productivity. A good place to start would be to stop rolling out the red carpet for the BSF of their Senior Leaders.

'Let's not say a word if it isn't true.'

– FONTAINES D.C.

The five pillars of Leadership and Teams

I want to introduce you to the five key pillars that, when done well, enable leaders and teams to be who they want to be and not be led by their BSF. They are:

1. It Always Starts With You
2. Trust
3. Emotional Intelligence
4. Culture
5. Leadership Conversations

These pillars of leadership and teams have been identified from years of working with different leaders and teams who were infected by their individual and collective BSFs. They embody my no BS approach and are what I build my coaching work on. They always succeed in shutting down the BSF. Some leaders and teams need to work on all of them, whereas others have specific opportunities to develop in one particular area.

We will first look at each of these in terms of when the BSF is preventing them from being effective. We will then look at them in more detail when I show you how leaders and teams can shut down their BSF and make these five pillars what your leadership and teams are built on.

1. It Always Starts With You

This is where you put your true, authentic self into your leadership and teams and make positive choices for how you want to work. Authentic leadership can be a breeding ground for BS as more and more people are commodifying it. Too much development of authentic leadership makes you fit a mould with other people telling you what your true, authentic self is. The only person who can tell *you* who *your* true, authentic self is is YOU. That's when you are at your most confident – when you know exactly who you are as your true, authentic self and you choose to be exactly that every single day at work.

This is why I am so passionate about helping you to Break the Mould as a leader and shut down your BSF. Your BSF loves to trick you into believing the BS and kidding yourself that you are being authentic when in fact you are still fitting a mould. It makes you think that you have to live up to your job title instead of what you stand for. You have to turn up to work as you, not your job title, and have that awareness to see through the perceptions of your BSF to work in reality and make the things that you want to happen, happen through decent human attitudes and behaviours. In the coaching work I do, the only thing I ever ask of the people I work with is to just be themselves and put that into their leadership and leave the BS behind for all the people who choose not to be their true, authentic selves.

Why your BSF fights this

Put simply, your BSF fights this because it doesn't want you to be your true, authentic self. It wants you to be a pale imitation of it and succumb to being your job title, accepting all the BS that comes with many leadership jobs. Your BSF wants you to get involved in office politics and waste your time and energy on corporate BS. It fights you making It Always Starts With You because your BSF knows that is where your strength is and where you can activate your greatest power to choose a positive response to your thoughts and feelings. This is where your armoury is; it's like where a superhero gets their superpower from because it is how you can choose to match your attitudes and behaviours to what you stand for as a decent human being, becoming your true authentic self along the way.

Winning the fight with your BSF

I saw the BSF in full-on action in this area when working with a Senior Leadership Team in a large organisation.

What was happening

This Senior Leadership Team had got themselves stuck in a rut. They were performing well yet had the lowest engagement scores that they had ever had and their teams were strung out through a real lack of direction and constant changes to how they worked. The senior leaders were allowing their BSFs to demonstrate immature behaviours that meant they were falling out with each other and working against each other instead of being joined up and leading their respective teams in a collaborative way.

Why I was hired

I was asked to go in and help them to be a high-performing team. My BSF radar warning system started when, during the briefing call, I was told, *"Help us sort them out, Tim. They need to really open up with each other and deal with their real problems."* This straight away told me that they needed to be helped to shut down their individual and collective BSF rather than be put through another off-the-shelf "how to be a high-performing team" training programme (trust me – that is what a lot of other coaches do, whilst leaving the BSF in full operation).

What happened

We set out on a six-month Team Coaching programme and when I started working with them, I noticed that they hid behind their job titles and "grades" instead of being the decent human beings that they are. They were also fixated on defending themselves and their teams even though they had nothing to defend against other than their own perceptions. And my God were they spouting a load of corporate BS. They were fixated on jargon and using processes to explain their attitudes and behaviours. It was like they were competing to show who knew the most about their organisation and what they did. Or at least what they purported to do.

I was staggered by how they spent so much time putting their hands up to speak as the conversation passed from one to another without any hint of action being taken. Their BSF was in hyperdrive so much that when I asked them what I thought was a simple question to trigger a conversation (*"What is High Performance for you as a team?"*) it was the catalyst for all-out war in a hotel meeting room.

They all had strong views on it and wanted even more vehemently to trash anything that their peers suggested. Imagine that: a Senior Leadership Team with over 120 years' combined leadership experience unable to agree on what High Performance is for their team. It's scary to think what their teams thought they were working towards if they couldn't discuss it without an argument. They were so lost in politics, defensive behaviour and a need to get in the first pre-emptive strike that we couldn't even have a conversation without disappearing down some irrelevant rabbit hole. There was a wall of negativity and apathy that I had to break down. Their BSF was telling them that they had to get the first shot in before someone else got a shot in at them.

Fixated on their negative thoughts and feelings, they couldn't get over the past issues that the BSF had woven such strong emotional ties to. And their self-image was definitely one of fearing someone else getting one over on them. This made them compete using their seniority and number of years of experience as leverage for getting what they wanted.

Some of the attitudes and behaviours that came out were so negative that it made me wonder how awful they were being to each other behind closed doors. Their apathy and resistance to change was clearly normal for them, so much so that they were oblivious towards how they were coming across to me who was there to help them.

They had no awareness of who they really were and who their peers really were. Their combined BSF loved this and kidnapped them by putting a bag over their heads and bundling them into the back of a van not knowing where they were going as a team. They resisted the coaching at first, using my questions as a chance to get one up on their peers and wasted time by simply taking turns sharing their opinions without anyone turning it into actions so they could change things for themselves.

How we shut down the BSF

I could see what was going on and called it out, introducing and explaining the BSF to them and how it was affecting them. I gave them some honest feedback on how they were coming across and my observations that they were allowing their previous run-ins and the culture they worked in to fuel their BSF. I played back to them what they were saying and challenged them to see things from the perspective of their teams and lift their heads from the deep, dark depths that their BSF was pushing them into.

I invited them to take a break from the BS they were up against and just go back to being their true, authentic selves. I created a safe space for them to leave their BSF out of the conversation and really get to know each other and choose for themselves how they wanted to work together. They discovered their values and beliefs via their Map of The World and shared this with each other. This led to revelations as they began to understand how they had behaved and became able to use those reflections to improve how they worked together. They tossed their job titles and grades into the bin and had open conversations as themselves. They shared some of their most difficult experiences in the team and gave each other honest feedback. We had a few tears and tantrums along the way that only strengthened their newfound bond as a team.

I coached them to raise their self-awareness to its maximum and helped them to empower themselves to be stripped right back to their true, authentic selves. This shut down their BSF for them and cleared the air so they could confidently go and lead their respective teams. They chose "ACTIONS NOT OPINIONS" as their motto and went on to not only agree what High Performance would be for their team but to also go and achieve it for the next twelve months. At the end of the programme, they left the same hotel meeting room feeling very relieved that they were no longer in a political war with each other and they all felt confident and keen to keep having open and honest conversations with each other.

We got back together six months later for an accountability session and it was like working with different people. They now had smiles on their faces and couldn't wait to tell me about the progress they had made. They complimented me by telling me that they now asked each other *"What would Tim say?"* when they needed to move to actions or were at risk of allowing the BSF to fire up again.

Their approach to putting your true, authentic self into your leadership and making positive choices to shut down your BSF can best be summed up by Michael, who was the most sceptical and critical member of that team when we first started working together. He told me mid-way through the Team Coaching programme that *"When we first started this, I would rather have ripped off one of my own arms than sit in here talking about myself. Now I can't wait for these sessions, Tim."*

'You can do it

It's just communication.'

– STONE FOUNDATION

2. Trust

Trust is the foundation that all leaders and teams must be built on. Without it you've got nothing. It doesn't always have to be peak trust, just enough to make leaders and teams have each other's backs and rely on each other to do their jobs and speak up at the right time. Trust is the magic sauce for creating psychological safety for you and your team. It is what enables you and your team to do the good jobs that you go to work to do.

The first rule of trust is to talk about trust. It often gets taken for granted and we just expect it to exist as we assume that people will behave in the way we want them to. As this book has shown so far, workplaces across the world are full of people who do not behave in the way you want them to! The way you can encourage people to behave the way you want them to is by building trust with them. But not in the way that the BS on a Google search tells you. Sure, there are some universal and practical things that build trust. What I help you with is to do the things that so many leaders don't do to build trust up to the level that you and your team need it to be at to be your best. Trust is a two-way street. I want you to build the level of trust with your team so you can speak to each other like you would your best mates down the pub.

The golden rules in my coaching for building trust are: -

- You must choose to trust your team to do a good job. You have to think that they can do it.
- You must role model what you expect from others.
- You must accept that people need different things to build trust with them – find out what your team needs from you to build trust with them. And then tell them what you need from them.
- You must show integrity in your actions.

Trust is always on the edge of the BS precipice as people can weaponise it or play the *"you need to earn my trust first"* card which puts people off ever building trust with you. The way I coach leaders is to remove the BS and allow trust to do what it does best – flourish and empower people to make positive choices.

Why your BSF fights this

Your BSF is not a fan of trust. It doesn't want you to trust yourself, never mind anyone else. Yet we all need trust as human beings. We all know how it feels when people do trust us and conversely when people break our trust. For leaders and teams, trust can be very black and white. Your BSF makes you take trust for granted and just expects that everyone will do the things that build trust with you without ever talking about it. You see, trusting others and it being reciprocated makes you feel safe and like you can achieve anything. That trust fires up the ability of leaders and teams to talk openly and work together to solve their problems. That is your BSF's worst nightmare. It will fight tooth and nail to stop people working together positively. You see this in leaders who bemoan their team not doing the things that build trust with them whilst also choosing not to role model those things themselves. Your BSF much prefers the *"do as I say, not as I do"* approach that does nothing to build trust amongst leaders and teams.

This can be best represented by when a leader starts to do their team's job for them even though they haven't given them a chance to show that they can be trusted to do it in the first place. Leaders can easily be swayed by the BSF's need for control and makes them lead through self-interest, thinking they need to have all the answers, to control the outcomes and solve everyone else's problems for them. The BSF is great at making leaders misunderstand the difference between "being a martyr" and doing the right thing.

Winning the fight with your BSF

I saw this thriving in Damien, who was an Exec Coaching client of mine. They had set up their own thriving business and they had even recruited a CEO to take over from them and lead the business moving forward.

What was happening

Damien was driven by "phone anxiety", where he couldn't stop checking his phone for calls and emails because he didn't trust his teams to do the work that he had previously done in setting up the business. It can best be described as "White Knight Syndrome", where the BSF confuses your human desire to help other people with not trusting people to do their jobs for themselves and makes you think that you have to ride in on your white horse to save the day. In reality, what people really want is the chance to build trust with you by doing a great job at what you employed them to do.

Damien couldn't stay out of the day-to-day work of his teams and was always getting involved where they didn't need to as their BSF told them that they were the only ones who had the requisite knowledge and ability to do a lot of important work. Damien's BSF doing this also made him forget that he had brought in a very capable and personable CEO to alleviate the pressure on him and allow him to focus on his true passion of Product Development. Instead, he was still here, there and everywhere breaking trust with anyone he came into contact with as he jumped in and did the things that others were there to do.

Why I was hired

Luckily, their strong-willed CEO, whom I knew from a previous organisation, gave Damien the tough love that he needed and introduced him to me as a Coach with the strong instruction to *"Go and spend time working on yourself instead of stopping others doing their work."*

What happened

We embarked on a twelve-month 1-2-1 coaching programme and, from our very first meeting, it was clear to me that Damien didn't trust the people in his business and hadn't done enough to build that trust with them or for them to trust in him. He talked incessantly about other people and how they should do their jobs. It was obvious that his BSF had him trapped in the *"don't trust others"* cupboard and, whilst Damien thought he needed *"help with my time management"*, I could see that he had the opportunity to learn how to trust others to do a good job.

At the right moment, I asked Damien *"all these people you keep talking about – why do they work here?"* I knew his BSF wouldn't like the direct challenge to how it was blaming others for getting too involved himself. Damien, whilst at first taken aback, understood what my question was really asking and he started to open up about how he found it difficult to let go because he felt so precious about the work that people did in his business. He felt a strong sense of pride and was afraid to trust others to do a good job because any of their failures would reflect on him and the brand he had worked so hard to build.

I asked Damien what the bigger failure would be, *"bring people in and not let them do a good job or try to do everything yourself?"* This set us off on a path of him taking a step back to learn more about how he could trust others to do a great job.

We explored what Damien needed other people to do to build trust with him and it was like a revelation as he realised that he needed to role model those things to others so they could reciprocate. We engaged with a number of his direct reports and peers and asked them for 360° verbatim feedback on the impact Damien had on them, using powerful questions, such as *"What do you want me to stop doing?"*, *"Tell me something you think I don't want to hear?"* and *"What do you need from me to know that I trust you?"*

I will never forget the afternoon that Damien and I spent reviewing his feedback and seeing the change in him as he realised the impact that his previous approach was having on the people around him. It also reminded him how important those people were to him and how much he wanted them to succeed and enjoy what they did.

How we shut down the BSF

From his coaching, Damien was able to take a different approach to how he engaged with people. He started to ask them open questions so he could understand what they were working on and give him the confidence to trust them. He instigated regular feedback conversations and started to show people how he appreciated their hard work. He also started to speak more at company meetings and shared his coaching journey and the changes he was making. This demonstration of vulnerability from Damien shifted everyone's perception of him from micromanaging them and never getting off their backs to a "human being".

I held Damien accountable over the course of his coaching programme to make sure he stayed consistent with putting his trust in others. When he had the odd wobble we focused on how he could choose a positive response to his "White Knight" BSF-influenced thoughts and feelings. I consistently challenged Damien to work hard on recognising the triggers for him jumping in and helped him to create new responses to his triggers that made him either stay out of it completely or offer his help and guidance to others so they could do it for themselves. Damien spent twelve months working with me, getting off his horse and being his own hero instead of trying to be everyone else's hero that no-one needed.

In a real moment of building trust, Damien sent me a WhatsApp message with capitalisation for maximum effect one day in between coaching sessions telling me *"I DID IT. I have just been to a meeting and did nothing but listen. AND IT WORKED. I came out with nothing else to do. Ha (smiley face emoji, thumbs up emoji)"*. He now felt able to be present without having to always come up with solutions and instead he could enjoy others coming up with their own solutions to help his business. All of this came from choosing to trust others. That was from someone who created a million-pound business from nothing through their own hard work and passion for creating new products. He just needed to shut down his BSF to stop him from interfering in other people's jobs!

'And the way I feel just makes me want to scream.'

– JAMES

3. Emotional Intelligence

Let's remember that Emotional Intelligence is how you recognise, understand and choose a positive response to your thoughts and feelings. It is how you choose your attitudes and behaviours to be your best version of you. Now imagine a team that has that combined ability. Every team member is at their best and able to respond to the conflict and challenges that arise when people come together as a team. No grudges are held and nothing is off limits in terms of how open and vulnerable they can be with each other. Then throw in an emotionally intelligent leader who doesn't take out their shitty moods on the team, who is tuned into how others are feeling and what they need from them. When you build an emotionally intelligent team, it will take you as close as you can get to experiencing utopia at work.

When it comes to emotional intelligence, you must see it as the key to unlocking your armoury to win the fight against your BSF. It is not just a "one off" to do an e-learning course on and think you have mastered it. It feeds everything you need to be the leader and team you want to be. Emotional intelligence can get a bad rap because it uses the word "emotional" which for the BSF is a red flag and some leaders still run a mile from it convinced that other people are the problem. When this happens, leaders end up avoiding the things that really make a difference, like giving difficult feedback because it feels awkward. My coaching helps you to tackle things head on and to develop and apply your emotional intelligence to do so.

Why your BSF fights this

Emotional Intelligence is the "elephant in the office" as it gets easily ignored. Your BSF makes you look for more practical solutions to the problems that leaders and teams face because it doesn't want you to realise that the key to your success lies in being able to choose a positive response to your thoughts and feelings. Your BSF wants to control you and make you react in an emotionally charged way. It fights against you talking about how you think and feel with others and just wants you to focus on the transactional part of your work rather than empower yourself to be transformational in how you and your team work.

Winning the fight with your BSF

A big part of my coaching work is facilitating Enthuse Your Leadership development programmes. This puts emotional intelligence at the heart of how leaders have an impact on their teams. One that will always stick with me was with an organisation that asked me to work with a cohort of their Senior Leaders and help them to engage with their teams differently, to address the silos and blame culture that were starting to infiltrate how their leaders and teams worked together.

What was happening

A lack of emotional intelligence meant that the BSF was making the leaders do whatever their thoughts and feelings told them to do – that BSF promised land of reactive auto-pilot. Their BSF was running the show. The leaders were taking their emotions out on their teams and peers. One such example given to me of this was how good they all were at being "keyboard warriors" sending each other shitty e-mails accusing others of doing something wrong. They were masters of slagging each other off behind their backs and not having any of the honest conversations that they needed to have. All this contributed to leading teams that had no initiative and were never trusted to be delegated to show any discretionary effort. This all left the leaders in a constant tiz of their own making where they were reacting to their emotions and putting themselves in a vicious circle of frustration, broken relationships and having too much to do.

Why I was hired

The leaders' BSF had created a toxic blame culture in which people tried to hide their own mistakes and avoid doing the things that they are not very good at to avoid the perceived risk of being "the one who gets it in the neck". I was asked to help them to recognise that the best thing to do was take a step back and work together on finding out what really happened and what really needed to be "fixed". Their self-preservation had turned into passive-aggression instead of holding their hands up to their own mistakes or asking people how they could help them when they made a mistake. And the odd thank you and positive recognition of a job done well were rarer than rocking horse shit as the BSF scripted the *"they don't do it for me so why should I do it for them?"* attitude.

The Head of L&D at the organisation was leading on changing the culture and was really keen to help their Senior Leaders to set the tone for their teams. They impressed on me how the leaders were good people and needed support to empower themselves to change. One of the most striking things the CEO said to me was, *"These people are not dickheads. They are behaving like dickheads and have been let down by other people and things here. They need some self-love and space to go back to being brilliant."*

What happened

I worked with a cohort of 12 Senior Leaders on a 9-month Enthuse Your Leadership programme, which blended face-to-face and virtual workshops with 1-2-1 coaching. This blended approach challenged the group as they had to be present at all sessions which in itself organically developed their emotional intelligence as they chose to manage distractions and focus on themselves rather than retreating to the comfort zone of sending e-mails and telling people what to do. The programme explored all capabilities of emotional intelligence and I used a group coaching approach to make it about the people in the room and their "real world" rather than theory and *"emotional bumfluff"* as one of the more outspoken leaders called it at the start of the programme.

I exposed these senior leaders, who took pride in holding others to account and micromanaging the life out of people and things, to their own thoughts and feelings and how it was impacting on them. A real breakthrough was when they started to understand more about their own perceptions and how they were reacting to them even though many could be proved to be false or were at least unproven. They dropped the bravado and were vulnerable with each other, sharing their insecurities and fears and helping each other to overcome them. It was great seeing them getting immersed in the programme and choosing to support each other and take action to change.

The workshops and coaching sessions were facilitated in a way to break down barriers by sharing honest feedback. The group committed to working together, which they now thought was preferable to "winning" at all cost. They lapped up the interactive parts of the workshops where their leadership was put to the test. I deliberately facilitated the workshops in a way that would break down barriers and force them to choose a positive response to their thoughts and feelings.

How we shut down the BSF

Each leader took their learning back to their teams and facilitated conversations that started to change their culture. They became leaders with emotional intelligence. They started to ask *"what happened?"* instead of their blame-loving BSF jumping in with *"who did that?"*

One of the senior leaders on the programme, Denise, was a beacon of the BSF holding back her emotional intelligence. When I spoke about self-management, she told me and her peer group how her team *"pushed all my wrong buttons"*. It was all them. She blamed her inability to self-manage her emotions on her team. Denise also shared that her biggest bone of contention is when she walks into work in the mornings and her team are *"all sat around having a brew and chatting"* and how that really sets her off for a bad day.

I wanted to give Denise the chance to work through this and asked her what she does when she sees her team in the mornings. She said she doesn't confront them or give them feedback, but she does send one or two of them an e-mail to ask them where they are up to with a piece of work. I went brave here in reminding her that her *"buttons"* are her buttons and that she has to take responsibility for them. No-one else is purposely pushing them for her as they don't know that spending a bit of time together first thing in the morning is something that pisses her off. I challenged her to remember that *"if people don't know what they're doing, how can they change what they do?"*

Denise was receptive to this and her peers encouraged her and empathised with her frustrations. I took the opportunity to use Denise as an example of how they could all shut down their BSF and grow their emotional intelligence. I asked Denise what she does in the mornings before she comes into work – whether she takes her dog for a walk or goes to the gym or listens to a podcast (i.e. things that can help her to choose positive emotions). She said she had breakfast with her husband and then drove to work, using the journey to ring her daughter, mum or sister on the way into the office. I asked her what those conversations were usually about and Denise became very demonstrative about how *"They just want to moan about everything that happened yesterday and how bad their day ahead was going to be, which then makes me moan about what I'm doing and…"* Denise tailed off as the penny dropped and her BSF retreated and she realised how those phone calls were putting her in a bad mood before she even got to work and, no matter what her team were doing, she was probably going to have her *"wrong buttons"* pressed.

Denise slumped a little bit into her chair and said, *"I need to stop making those calls, don't I?"* Her tone and the look on her face said, *"I already knew this and I now realise how stupid I am being"*. Your BSF is very good at making you look stupid and wants leaders and teams to forget about their emotional intelligence so you can only react badly to your negative emotions.

When Denise returned to a later workshop, she breezed into the room and took great delight in telling her peers how she had stopped the moany phone calls and now went into work feeling totally comfortable about what her team are doing. She had shifted her focus to how they were performing rather than trying to see a problem. Denise talked about how she was now pushing her *"right buttons"* and not taking her moods or frustrations out on others. She eulogised about how this had transformed how she felt about work and, in turn, encouraged her team to be more open with her rather than trying to avoid her wrath just for having a cup of tea in the morning!

'Wish somebody'd make my mind up
Oh, don't leave me in charge
of my own heart.'

– TOM GRENNAN

"Your BSF is very good at making you look stupid"

4. Culture

Your culture is the "deal breaker" for leaders and teams. You can achieve the best results ever but, if you feel like the culture you work in is not right, then those results will mean nothing to you. Your culture is how it feels to work where you work. This impacts on your sense of belonging and self-motivation to do a good job. When your culture is right, you and your team can overcome any challenge you face. When your culture is wrong, your BSF will have a field day.

This is the "big one" – all roads lead to Culture and it can't be built in a day. Culture is something that all organisations talk about and want but it is often too intangible or too big a problem for them to do something truly impactful.

A lot of culture work gets lost in the Corporate BS as, instead of building the culture that people really want, we stick posters of values on the office wall and insist that everyone uses the same "culture branded" background on Teams. All of it is done with positive intent but actually serves to make the culture feel contrived, which powers the collective BSF. Organisations sometimes blow a massive budget on culture work and it leads to nothing changing.

The way I coach leaders and teams to build their culture means that it is done in a way that puts people in control and makes them responsible for their attitudes and behaviours. They can't blame Corporate BS for stopping them from working how they want to work, meaning they have to work together to build and own their own Culture.

Why your BSF fights this

Culture is something that your BSF excels at destroying and hoodwinks you into believing that it is completely out of your control. The culture of leadership and teams comes from how it feels to work with leaders and in your teams. It's not about the fancy initiatives that are supposed to drive culture or the perks or working somewhere, it is about pure unadulterated human emotions.

We want our work culture to feel positive, inclusive, compassionate and purposeful. Your BSF wants your culture to feel negative, exclusive, heartless and pointless, so it retains its hold over you and makes you feel like a victim rather than feeling empowered. It often succeeds too as leaders and teams succumb to the seductive work of your BSF making you think that you can't change anything or that culture is something that just happens and doesn't need any work on building it.

I am specifically talking here about the "Local Culture" of leadership and teams. The organisational culture is the "Global Culture" and very few leaders and teams can truly influence the whole organisation. Many try and fail and the BSF makes them give up, leaving the culture to chance and getting the adverse effect that they set out to achieve. The best place for leaders and teams to work on their culture is in their Local Culture, which is always in your control. Your Local Culture is where it's at for leaders and teams because that is nurtured through the impact you have on others and how you work together. That is determined by your attitudes and behaviours which, when you choose a positive response to your BSF, are always 100% in your control.

Everyone who joins your Local Culture brings expectations based on their previous emotional experiences in other Local Cultures. If they come from a positive experience, they have high expectations and will be disappointed very quickly at any sign of BS. Their BSF will trigger telling them that they have made a mistake joining your team and will negatively impact their ability to settle in and contribute. If they come from a negative experience, they will have low expectations and be on the lookout for the same things. Their BSF will rapidly create a perception of validating that they are in the same negative culture as before and the negative traits that they showed in that culture will quickly surface.

Your Local Culture is the product of your attitudes and behaviours. You need awareness of what you want it to be and to use that to take action in creating it. Your BSF wants you to leave it to chance and stop you from holding each other to account when you show the attitudes and behaviours that you don't want in your Local Culture. It will also gag you from ever sharing positive reinforcement when your peers demonstrate the attitudes and behaviours you do want in your Local Culture. It's one of the reasons why so much money gets wasted on organisations and teams choosing their values only for them to just become something that gets stuck on the office wall and website. No-one ever raises them when their Local Culture starts to slip. Your BSF makes you leave the values as just words that no-one can ever remember or understand.

Winning the fight with your BSF

I had a fantastic experience working with a Senior Leadership Team who needed help to build their Local Culture and implement it with their teams across the organisation.

What was happening?

They were working in silos and were guilty of petty arguments amongst themselves whilst avoiding the tough conversations with each other. They had never done any work on their culture, and it showed. Their arguments and the awkwardness from them avoiding each other cascaded back throughout the business.

There was a real risk of cliques forming in their leadership team and across their wider teams. Their BSF had them believing that they only worked well with peers who were alike in their personalities and preferred leadership approach. This was making it increasingly difficult to build their desired culture and there was concern about their ability to attract and retain new talent into the business. It was also becoming quite exhausting for them as emotions often ran high in their interactions with each other, including in front of other people, and cliques had started to form.

Why I was hired

The Head of HR and Managing Director recognised that they needed to do something and wanted to make sure that what they did had an impact and wasn't just a "management training programme". They were keen to use the straight-talking language that they were comfortable with and did not want to do anything that forced them to become "more corporate". It was vital to them that they had someone to facilitate them having positive conflict and opening up some difficult conversations in a way that no-one felt left out or blamed. That led to relationships being rebuilt and the firm establishment of accountability for their culture.

What happened?

We set out on a 10-month Team Coaching programme with five workshops addressing specific areas. They also completed peer-to-peer 360° verbatim feedback and 1-2-1 coaching which led to open conversations between those peers who had the biggest challenges to overcome with each other. A Team Assessment was completed which highlighted some key areas that needed improving, including giving each other honest feedback, their communication with each other and their willingness and ability to have positive conflict with each other.

There was a real sense of them needing to "clear the air" with each other. I got them to contract with each other and agree on how they would work with each other at the workshops and how they would call each other out if any of them demonstrated the things that they committed to "We Will Not Do". This was transferred to their interactions and they all practised calling each other out when any negative or antagonistic attitudes or behaviours were present. This led to in-the-moment feedback and open discussions replacing grudges being held.

One of the biggest things that happened was them all realising that, in order to create the culture they wanted, they had to role model what they wanted in that culture. "Role modelling" became a phrase that was repeated, and not once did they use it with any hint of sarcasm or it being overused. They all collectively bought into this idea and worked hard on developing themselves in order to develop the culture and how they impacted on their teams.

They were genuinely one of the best groups I have ever worked with and were like a collective sponge lapping up the learning they got from the sessions. They were all keen to make their culture what they want it to be.

How we shut down the BSF

For all their enthusiasm, I recognised that we still needed to get something specific out in the open to help them shut down their BSF and Break the Mould that was setting in. I gave them brutal feedback on how, despite them now working better together, they had still not really nailed something in terms of what really had to change in their culture.

This came to a head at their workshop where we specifically addressed the silos that were present and a few BSFs started to re-appear. It was like Whack-a-Mole as different BSFs popped up around the room, pointing fingers at their peers instead of suggesting how to move forward. Whilst they were all respectful of each other and had a high level of rapport, their collective BSF was stopping them from getting to the point of what needed to change.

They admitted that they would use "banter" to discuss things instead of being really honest and putting out what they really felt like. This was limiting the tangible action they took as a result of their Team Coaching sessions despite them all committing to individual and team actions. As another game of BSF tennis commenced, and more fingers were pointed and defensiveness crept in, I stepped in and asked, *"What are the actual consequences of what you are talking about? What actually happens as a result of these things that you are raising against each other?"* Some of the group looked at me with a quizzical expression and others suddenly found the pattern in the carpet really interesting.

The Managing Director gave me an optimistic glance and then looked around the room, wanting someone to speak up. He gave it a few more seconds of silence before stepping up and saying, *"I'll tell you what the consequences are Tim... fuck all. It is all 'wooden dollars' that we're trying to protect."* This was a massive statement and brought people back to the table. The MD led an impassioned conversation about how important it was to change their culture, reminding everyone about how good a job they were already doing. They were leading a successful business and their opportunity was much more about enhancing what they did rather than fixing something.

This shut down their BSFs once and for all and completely changed them as a team as they all worked even harder to bring their Local Cultures to life, starting with how they worked as a Senior Leadership Team. Their relationships flourished and they went from avoiding tough conversations to relishing making their conversations with each other really open and honest. They took responsibility for their Local Cultures and for their role in making sure that they fostered the right feelings in everyone whilst they were at work.

'Talking bullshit, bullshit, bullshit
Bullshit, bullshit
I want to know, I want to know.'

– BLACK GRAPE

5. Leadership Conversations

Leaders and teams are nothing without having the right conversations. Our ability to communicate is how we are understood and how we understand others. It is the heartbeat of a successful workplace. Your impact and the relationships you build come from the conversations that you have. No-one's impact comes from being able to write a succinct e-mail. Your relationships can't just be about "who you know not what you know". As a leader, all you're ever doing is having conversations.

My coaching brings those conversations to life by helping leaders to make them just that – a conversation, a chat between two human beings. You don't need models and theories or "How tos" to have a great conversation. It's innate, you know how to do this, it's just your BSF getting in the way. You just need you and the confidence to shut down your BSF so it can't prevent you from having the desired positive impact in your conversations. I take leadership conversations from being something that you "have to do" to constant opportunities to engage your team and work together to make work what you want it to be.

Why your BSF fights this

Your BSF wants your conversations to be simple and without any risks being taken. Its fear of the unknown makes you want your conversations to be predictable and keep your arse firmly on the comfort zone bean bags. It tells you that your conversations are something to fear and that they take up too much time. It makes you expect everyone else to communicate in the same way that you do. It builds an internal picture of you already knowing what people are going to say and that your conversations are a waste of time because they will be repetitive. It really enjoys making you think that some conversations need to be prescribed by an appraisal form and that some things only belong in "formal" conversations. The BSF approach to conversations is the peak of the BS that leaders and teams face and allow themselves to fall victim to.

I use the term "Leadership Conversations" because that is what they are. They are conversations had by leaders with their teams. It is something that leaders need to take responsibility for and be accountable for making them happen. Too many leaders allow their BSF to make their conversations reactionary and don't bother to think proactively about the conversations they need to have with their teams. Only a BSF would tell leaders that feedback can be given twice a year or that they need to have a really tight agenda for their team meetings and not stray from it.

I don't know about you, but I don't remember what I did last week so giving me feedback on something I did last month is pointless. Meetings don't need an agenda, they need a purpose and, surely, the best conversations that we have are the ones where we have no idea what is going to happen.

Your BSF wants you to believe the BS that is spouted about Leadership Conversations as the world calls them "difficult" and "courageous". A conversation is just a conversation. And that goes for whether it is done face-to-face, over the telephone or on MS Teams. Your BSF is also a brilliant blocker to you being able to have conversations about your conversations and agreeing how to make them more effective. It wants you to leave your conversations to chance, allowing human emotions to get in the way and moving you away from positive action, but your conversations should be something that triggers positive emotional experiences and makes you want to keep having them.

Winning the fight with your BSF

One of my favourite coaching programmes to run is my Engaging Leaders programme which puts senior leaders through a series of workshops and 1-2-1 coaching that focuses on raising their self-awareness and choosing the impact they want to have in their conversations. I run this programme every year with a global organisation, and how one particular leader changed their conversations with their team will stay with me forever.

What was happening

Before the first cohort, the senior leadership population were very well thought of and considered "the future execs". They consistently performed well and led teams that grew the business and delivered on projects. They had all previously completed leadership development and had individual goals and personal development plans in place. What was missing was how they engaged with their teams and peers. Whilst there was no massive level of negativity there, there was a big opportunity to help the senior leaders to become the leaders they wanted to be and to role model open and honest conversations by going beyond the "corporate" and transactional conversations that could be commonplace.

Why was I hired?

To help the senior leaders to go on a development journey (yes, I know *"journey"* is a bit of a wanky word but bear with me) that enabled them to engage their teams and peers in a different way. One of the key purposes of the programme was to give the leaders the space to have the conversations with each other that they weren't yet having with their teams. This meant they could give more effective feedback and be able to have really frank, open conversations about their impact. This would then give them the confidence to go and have them back in the "real world" whilst benefiting from the impact they would have.

The Head of Talent and Development (Hey, Emma Lidgett) wanted a coach to lead on this programme so it developed the emotional intelligence and authenticity of the leaders rather than being another "how to have a leadership conversation" programme.

What happened?

We launched the Engaging Leaders programme and Emma and I co-facilitated three two-day face-to-face workshops with me delivering virtual workshops in between that acted as the "kick up the arse" to implement their learning. Each leader also completed 1-2-1 coaching sessions that gave them the chance to explore their individual development needs and be challenged to take action that made a difference.

Emma and I are the perfect "tag team" as I lead on the emotional intelligence and authentic leadership development and Emma provided the real context of the organisation, pushing them to make changes for themselves and not use excuses like *"it's always been that way"* or *"we're not allowed to do that here"*. We also put them through their paces with interactive activities that push their BSF to its limits – if being blindfolded in front of your peers doesn't push you out of your comfort zone then nothing will!

As the first programme started, some of the group were resistant and had the demeanour of *"we've done all this before"* whilst others were reticent to be really open with their peers as their culture was one where being competitive could be really rewarding. You could see in their body language sometimes that their BSF was telling them to reject the coaching and go back to doing what felt safe and "normal" to them.

I was relentless in bringing them back to looking at themselves and my motto of "It Always Starts With You" was one that a few probably felt like they had had tattooed on them by the end of the programme! And it worked. Despite some initial scepticism, the senior leaders started to change their conversations with their teams, using some of the resources from the programme to facilitate open and honest conversations with their teams. They also started to make more subtle changes, like asking their teams what they wanted to get from their meetings and 1-2-1's instead of being led by static agendas that had long passed their use-by date.

They lapped up the journey (I told you to bear with me!) of self-discovery and came back to the workshops keen to re-engage in the honest conversations with each other, holding each other to account for being their authentic selves. Each leader is asked to present on their own journey at the end of the programme and a red thread of those presentations was *"When we started this programme, I was cynical and didn't expect anything to change. Having done it and focused on myself, I can see the difference it has made for me and my team. Now I am not scared of any conversation that I need to have."* All of the group demonstrated their ability to change their behaviour by choosing a positive response to their thoughts and feelings.

How we shut down the BSF

One of the best ways to shut down your BSF is to have the conversations that you and your teams really need to have. The most striking example from that first programme is Lisa, who at the start of the programme suggested that her friends and family would describe her as a *"dragon"* at work. Lisa was very honest that she found some of her team difficult and had a desire for them to change themselves rather than consider how she needed to change herself first.

Lisa worked really hard on choosing a positive response to the thoughts and feelings that were turning her into the perceived "dragon" and opened up more and more as the programme progressed. She also challenged herself to speak up more even though, internally, her BSF would tell her to stay quiet and stir BS telling her that her peers weren't interested in what she had to say.

As part of the programme, I encouraged the group to drop the "corporate" approach to some of their conversations and instead look for opportunities to talk about how people are really feeling. Then they could work on getting their perceptions out of the way, engaging with people in a way that had a positive impact for them as leaders.

Lisa took this challenge on and then some. She had been very open about a particular member of her team who caused her some consternation, and with whom her conversations had fallen into being awkward and formal, which didn't remove any of the challenges between them. Some of this was fuelled by the team member having applied for the job that Lisa had got. We know how a BSF loves to stir that into negative shit that makes us distrust each other and hold our disappointment against a peer. Lisa shared how she had dreaded working with this person for the last 12-18 months.

In her end of programme presentation, Lisa told the story of how she had chosen to change the conversations with this member of her team by opening up about how she was thinking and feeling and inviting them to respond so they could move on. Lisa bravely shared with her team member how she was losing sleep over worrying about the conversations that they needed to have and how she didn't trust them or feel like they trusted Lisa.

And her team member opened up like never before. Telling Lisa that she did not want her to feel like that, she agreed that they both needed to do more to build trust. They agreed on what needed to change and how they would both do that. They also agreed to follow up on their conversation, keeping their future interactions open and honest.

Lisa told her peers how her courage in taking this approach to her conversations came from choosing a positive response to her thoughts and feelings. She also shared how this opened the door to facilitating a Team Day where all of her team engaged in some of the conversations from the programme, like contracting for the attitudes and behaviours they wanted from each other and exploring their respective Map of the World. Lisa's action enabled the previously difficult team member to be someone who contributed to those conversations and showed a keenness to work with Lisa.

Lisa summed it up perfectly: *"It's not about words; it's about understanding"*. Your BSF doesn't want you to understand you or others. It only wants you to understand what negative BS it expects you to think, feel and say. Lisa is a shining example of what happens when you positively respond to that BS and have the conversations that you want to have.

'Take some time to make some sense
Of what you want to say.'

– OASIS

It can be different for Leaders and Teams

It doesn't have to be like the bad examples I have shared in this chapter for your leadership and your teams. I'm sure you have read some of those examples and can relate to them being similar to your experiences and the experiences of others.

It can be different, and you can be like the leaders and teams who have shut down their BSF. You don't have to go on in the same way if your BSF has hammered your leadership and teams previously. You can change it for you and for your team. It takes hard work and commitment to shut down your BSF, but the path that you want to follow is on the other side of shutting it down.

To stay motivated as a leader and with your teams, consider how much it must cost when your BSF takes over. How many resources your BSF must waste. How much progress is hampered by your BSF deciding what happens next. Instead of that, choose to put your money, time and resources into shutting down your BSF.

All these companies who have "Don't be a Dick" painted on their walls need to replace it with "Don't let your Bullshit Factory win".

'Maybe I could use a hand
I must admit I'm out of bright
Ideas to keep the hell at bay
Distractions only last a day
The night is so impossible
But I'm damned if I give up tonight.'

– SAM FENDER

What have we done in this chapter?

- ➡ Called out the BS that seeps into leadership and teams
- ➡ Shown how the BSF can make people turn away from telling the truth
- ➡ Highlighted how the BSF can ruin work for people
- ➡ Explored the five pillars of Authentic Leadership
- ➡ Witnessed real-life examples of the BS that gets in the way of leaders and teams being who they want to be
- ➡ Introduced you to how I can help leaders and teams to shut down their BSG

Coaching questions to shut down your BSF in your leadership and teams...

- ➡ How can you drop your job title and be your true, authentic self?
- ➡ Where does the BSF impact on your leaders and teams?
- ➡ What are you doing to build trust?
- ➡ How can you make sure that you never take your shitty moods out on other people?

- When do you need to shut down your BSF as a leader?
- What do you need to do to build your Local Culture?
- How effective are your Leadership Conversations?
- How can I help you and your teams to shut down your BSF and be who you want to be?

CHAPTER SIX

CONCLUSION

'But you never know until you try
How things just might be.'

– THE STYLE COUNCIL

Congratulations on completing the book and starting to show your BSF that it has a battle on its hands. You have given yourself a head start on that constant battle with your BSF. And it is now a battle that you are ready to win.

The book is just the start of your journey towards achieving freedom of thought and being in control of how you respond to your feelings. You now have some DIY techniques and tools to practise using in the real world. I have no doubt you will start to see the difference.

Yet, this book is just round one. You're now ready to take the next step because the book has primed you with an awareness of your BSF and the fun techniques that you can apply every day to shut it down. But that is not the end of it. Far from it. You have to take the head start you have given yourself and make sure you keep going.

Remember that getting complacent is exactly what your BSF wants you to do. It knows you've read this book and is sitting there with its hand wavering over the "START" button to its production line. You now have to take what you've learned and turn it into consistent practice to make sure you can always hit that big red "STOP" button quickly.

The most important thing you have achieved already is enhancing your awareness of your BSF and taking on the challenge to shut it down. Make sure you don't allow your BSF to file this book under "another book I've read and forgotten" and remember the hard graft you have put in just from getting through all the reflections and activities. You have:

- Witnessed how the BSF sabotages decent people into becoming rude and argumentative.
- Delved deep into the workings of your BSF and learned both how it works and the threats it poses to you.
- Read my own story and seen how close I came to letting my BSF ruin my life.
- Started to build up your armoury in the battle against your BSF with the techniques in Chapter 4.
- A much better awareness and understanding of how the BSF can ruin leaders and teams and have real-world examples to consider putting into action to prevent the BSF from turning you into a shitty leader and your team into a collective BSF.

WHAT HAPPENS NEXT?

Subscribe at my website or follow me on LinkedIn.

www.enthusecoaching.com

https://www.linkedin.com/in/timrobertsenthuse/

I regularly share blogs and newsletters to help you to keep shutting down your BSF.

You can listen to the Spotify playlist for the book by scanning the QR code below:

And don't forget to head to my website where you can download the worksheet for the book with the coaching questions so you can shut down your Bullshit Factory for good. Scan the QR code to head to my website:

More importantly....

Your BSF won't go away just because you've finished the book, so you now need to choose what you do next to keep winning your battles. You can choose to put this book on your shelf to gather dust with all the other ones you have never done anything with, or you can go and practise the techniques and evolve your mindset to choose a positive response to shut down your BSF. The next stage of shutting your BSF down is what we do together – the "big stuff".

One of the challenges I've had writing this book is that the coaching work I do is so bespoke to the leaders and teams that I work with that it can't all be put in a single book that works for everyone.

The "big stuff" that I will do with you takes you from someone who is *"trying"* to shut down your BSF to someone who lives a BS-free life. Imagine how that would feel. Imagine how those you love and lead would feel. Imagine knowing you could not be derailed, no matter what happens in your day, as you have unlimited ways to positively respond to your thoughts and feelings. Check out the testimonials from some of my coaching clients at the end of the book to get a sense of the power that the "big stuff" gives you.

Maybe you're the senior leader whose BSF is stopping you from being brave enough to just be your true, authentic self?

Maybe you're a Senior Leadership Team who are stuck in a rut and need to open up and get to know each other better?

Maybe you're the leader who needs more confidence to fight your BSF in the big moments?

Maybe you're the leader who needs to stop pressing the wrong buttons and give your team more responsibility?

Maybe you're the "Work Wanker" and need to stop letting work take over your life?

Maybe you're the CEO who can't get off your "White Horse" to trust your team to do a good job?

Maybe you want the confidence to have the conversations that you need to have with your team?

Maybe you need to get your days off to a better start and stop letting your BSF ruin them for you and your team?

Maybe you're the Director who needs to move away from *"task, task, task"* and go back to finding joy and happiness in your work?

Maybe you work with your very own "Incompetent Ian" and need the strength to positively deal with their negative antics?

Maybe you're the HR Director who has a miserable sod on reception ruining your company culture?

Or

Maybe you just want to feel better about yourself?

Whatever you want, you need to be in the room with me and my loafers. We will have a much bigger impact together. Let's shut your BSF down together and make your hard work and positive intent all worth it. I can help you, your team and your organisation to take the concepts laid out in this book further and give you the days that you want at work and the life you want to live.

Book a call with me using the QR code and we will create the coaching solutions for your leaders and teams to solve the problems caused by their Bullshit Factories:

'Lookout kid, trust your heart
You don't have to play the part
they wrote for you
Just be true
There are things that you could do
That no one else on earth could ever do.'

– ARCADE FIRE

IT ALWAYS STARTS WITH YOU

Mental Health Support

NHS Talking Therapies

https://www.nhs.uk/mental-health/talking-therapies-medicine-treatments/talking-therapies-and-counselling/nhs-talking-therapies/

Andys Man Club

www.andysmanclub.co.uk

Mind

www.mind.org.uk/donate/

Heads Together

www.headstogether.org.uk

ACKNOWLEDGEMENTS

This is one of the hardest parts of writing a book! Because there are so many people who have helped me to shut down my BSF. And because even as I sit to write this, my BSF is telling me that people don't want me to mention them and that they only help me to get rid of me!

So I am role modelling one last time how to shut down your BSF ...

My first thanks have to go to the brilliant (and not so brilliant!) people whose stories are shared in the book. Without you, my work would be meaningless, and I would not have the opportunity to do what I love.

Especially my irascible receptionist mate from Chapter Two, without whom I would never have been able to write that story. I genuinely hope that one day you get to shut down your BS Factory and stop making life miserable for you and anyone else who meets you.

There are some people who must be given special mentions here as you have always supported me and challenged me to keep going. You see the joy that I get from what I do and the hard work I put in. You know who you are and now I can name-drop you, so the world knows your name: -

- Aimee Bateman
- Andrew Hibbert
- Andrew Stotter-Brooks
- Danielle Soens-Hughes
- Emma Lidgett
- Jules Darvill
- Karene Lamond
- Matt Grainger
- Nova Ferguson
- Rob Johnson
- Zoe Sinclair

I have to give the biggest name-drop to Leila Green, my writing coach, without whom I would not be achieving my lifelong ambition of writing books. And most importantly, writing them in the way I want to write them. How you put up with me, Leila, is beyond me! Thank you for always challenging me, always supporting me, always being honest with me and always, always reminding me to just be me. You are a huge inspiration. Thank you, Leila – I can't do it without you.

And finally, my biggest thanks go to my Mum, Dad, Our Kid and my best friends. None of whom will actually read this book! They don't need to because they don't need Tim Roberts, the Leadership Coach and Author, they just need Tim Roberts. They trust me to do what I do, never judge me, always support me and keep me smiling. The close group of family and friends that I have is one of life's greatest joys and proof that you will meet many people in your life, yet only truly great people will really matter to you, and it is those great people that keep you going and lift you up during the bad times. Thank you.

Have a good time all the time.

MORE PRAISE FOR TIM ROBERTS

"Tim was introduced to me by one of my most trusted friends when I asked if she knew any good coaches. She provided Tim's details to me, with a comment along the lines of 'he is a good guy and will not stand any of your BS'. Turns out Tim really is one of the good guys and I really enjoy working with him. Obviously, he doesn't stand any of my BS.

"Tim has really helped me tame my BSF and, whilst I am honestly exhausted by my self-management and daily care routines, I admit (sometimes very grudgingly) that this 'stuff' works and makes a huge difference to my wellbeing. Thanks Tim, you have helped me enormously. We have also laughed a lot as well, so that works for me.

"Tim has also worked with some of my senior management team. He has held us together and let us air our frustrations and blame (BSF alive and well) and then steered us gently into a better place. He has listened again and again and now steers us not so gently back to our shared purpose and areas we manage and influence. I think we have all individually turned down our BSF dial.

"Tim has also had feedback from one of our more robust managers, who relishes breaking people by his 'banter' and force of personality. The manager has said 'I like your choice Tania, he is ok. He stood up to me and that was ok'. Blimey Tim, that is praise beyond belief.

"Tim is always professional, looks smart and dresses well, swears a lot, though mainly in books rather than coaching sessions, to be honest. I love working with Tim and I hope we always stay in touch however our future worlds grow."

– TANIA PENNILL, DIRECTOR OF HR (AND ONE OF THE STARS OF THIS BOOK)

"I've always loved a bit of internal training – for the change from the BAU but mostly for the opportunity to have a bit of craic with some like-minded people. However, I was very much of the mindset that I've heard it all before, I've done it all before and it's really just a load of fluffy corporate rubbish. But two things happened as a result of my time with Tim. Firstly, he called me out on

my own BSF which was telling me that no one wanted to hear what I had to say (turns out they do!) and, secondly, he inspired and challenged me to be authentically me. I'd tried so hard to be what I thought a good leader should be – strong, decisive, devoid of emotions, able to handle anything that is thrown at me without a second thought. Tim helped me to see that being honest and vulnerable with my team and showing them my true self resulted in my team being honest and vulnerable with me, allowing us to move past some difficult situations, not with ease but with a sense of accomplishment and a job well done."

– LISA GIBNEY, HEAD OF OPERATIONS
(ANOTHER STAR OF THIS BOOK AND DEFINITELY NOT 'A DRAGON'!)

"'Keep smiling, keep being you' ...that's Tim's mantra. Although I've worked with Tim for a number of years, I've only recently come to realise the significance of these five little words. If we're not happy and not being ourselves and not working in a way that fits with our own values, beliefs and character, then what the fuck are we all doing?!!

"That's where Tim's way of coaching helps you to find the keys to your very own bullshit bulldozer so you can bring that negativity crashing down. This book explains just how to do that!"

– HAYLEY WARD, BRAND AND MARKETING DIRECTOR

"I've been working with Tim for around three years and his support and guidance has undoubtedly been a significant factor in the successes that I have had. It started with Tim – for me at least! Our time spent focussing on who I am, what matters to me, what motivates me, and most of all seeing that I am the only one who can do something about what is the biggest blocker to me being authentic, me! It's opened up and made visible what my own BSF was churning out: self-doubt, insecurities, imposter syndrome, and led me to overthink things time and time again. I see it now, it gets picked up on the BS Radar, and I shut it down. It does come back, wearing new guises or peddling the same old same old, it always will."

– STUART MORLAND, MANAGING DIRECTOR

Milton Keynes UK
Ingram Content Group UK Ltd.
UKHW042034111124
451050UK00001B/1

9 781915 850331